Keep An~~~~
On Amélie

A farce

Georges Feydeau

Translated and adapted by
Robert Cogo-Fawcett
and Braham Murray

Samuel French – London
New York – Toronto – Hollywood

KEEP AN EYE ON AMÉLIE

First presented at the Royal Exchange Theatre, Manchester (under the title *She's in Your Hands!**) on 28th June, 1990, with the following cast:

Amélie	Lorraine Ashbourne
Marcel	Richard McCabe
Étienne	Terence Beesley
Irene	Naomi Buch
Pochet	John Cording
Van Putzeboum	Colin Prockter
Koshnadieff	Peter Rutherford
The Prince of Palestrie	Sandor Elés
Charlotte ⎫ Palmyre ⎬	Hilary Tones
The Mayor	Edmund Kente
Mouilletu ⎫ Police Inspector ⎬	James Thackwray
Cornette	John Axon
Adonis	Tom Hudson
Bibichon	Tim McMullan
Boas	Luke Williams
Valcreuse	Tim Dutton
Yvonne	Rena Jugati
The Brat	Natalie Casey Dionne Clarke Katie Wilkinson
Florist's Assistants/Shop Assistants/Photographers	Paul Warren Leslie Hattersley

Directed by Gregory Hersov
Designed by Johan Engels

* This production was set in the round

CHARACTERS

Amélie Pochet, a cocotte
Palmyre ⎤
Yvonne ⎟
Bibichon ⎬ her friends
Boas ⎟
Valcreuse ⎦
Pochet, her father
Étienne de Milledieu, her lover
Adonis, her younger brother
Irene, a countess, Marcel's mistress
Marcel Courbois, Étienne's best friend
Koshnadieff, a general in the service of the Prince of
    Palestrie
Van Putzeboum, Marcel's German godfather
The Prince of Palestrie
Charlotte, Marcel's maid
Mouilletu ⎤
Cornette ⎦ Clerks of the Court
The Mayor
The Brat, a bridesmaid
A Police Superintendent
Florist's Boys, Shop Assistant, Photographers (all non-
    speaking)

ACT I   Amélie's salon

ACT II   Marcel's bedroom

ACT III   Scene 1   The Town Hall
             Scene 2   Amélie's bedroom

Time—Paris in the early 1900s

The original French title of *Keep An Eye On Amélie* is *Occupe-toi d'Amélie*

ACT I

Amélie's salon

Amélie is standing by the piano making her guests listen to the gramophone. Bibichon, with a cigar in his mouth is sitting between Palmyre and Yvonne on the sofa. Valcreuse and Boas are sitting at the card-table playing cards. The record being played is of Caruso singing "Di Quella Pira" from "Il Trovatore"

The CURTAIN *rises as Caruso sings the phrase "Marse Avvampo". As Caruso's voice rises on the thirteenth and fourteenth bars . . .*

Yvonne Oh yes.
Palmyre (*ecstatically*) Ah! Yes, yes.
Amélie Ouf! Unbelievable.
All A—A—Ah! (*They all listen*)
Bibichon Is that Caruso bawling?
Amélie Bawling?
Bibichon All right. Singing then. Not a bad voice.
Yvonne Be quiet.
Palmyre Yes. Be quiet.
Bibichon All right.

There is an almost religious silence. The women are in seventh heaven. The tenor holds a long high note on the twenty-fourth or twenty-fifth and everybody appears to hang on the lips of the absent singer almost in a trance for as long as the note lasts. When the singer continues Bibichon continues with him

(*Singing*) La, la, la, la, la.
All No, please. No. Not you.
Bibichon What?
Yvonne God did not bless your voice.
Palmyre Caruso doesn't need any accompaniment.
Bibichon I was just helping him out.
Yvonne Well don't. Let us listen in peace.
Bibichon I'm not stopping you.
Palmyre }
Yvonne } (*together*) Enough.
All Quiet.
Bibichon I was singing quietly.
All Shut up! (*They carry on ad lib in this fashion until the aria is concluded*)
Yvonne Will you be quiet!
Bibichon Sorry!

At last Bibichon is silent but the record is finished

Amélie That's it. It's over.
Palmyre (*to Bibichon*) And all we heard was Bibichon!
Bibichon At least I'm here in the flesh.
Amélie You think that's an advantage?
Valcreuse Have you got anything a little lighter?
Amélie "Selections from Racine" by Sarah Bernhardt?
All No!
Amélie Point taken.

Bibichon lights another cigar

Not another! Listen Bibichon, you're worse than a chimney. We can
hardly breathe in here.
Bibichon (*still lighting it*) It'll be the last one! No more after this!
Boas Quiet now, all of you. A toast.
Bibichon Good idea!
Yvonne Shush!
Amélie Who to?
Boas To you, dear lady.
Amélie Me? What have I done?
Boas Today is the first anniversary in your new profession. We must drink to
your success.
Valcreuse Ah, but wait. Amélie's father should be here too. Where is he?
Yvonne (*calling off*) Monsieur Pochet.

Pochet enters

Pochet Can I help?
Boas We were just about to drink a toast to celebrate your daughter's first
year in her new profession.
Pochet Oh, Amélie! This is the proudest moment of my life since I was on
traffic duty at the Place de la Concorde. I remember——
Amélie (*firmly*) You must tell Monsieur Bibichon later.
Bibichon Why do you always palm me off with old people. They're so
boring!
Boas To Amélie and her lov——
Amélie Patron!
Boas Patron, of course, who makes these soirées possible.

They drink

Pochet I'd just like to say a few words . . .
Amélie (*leading him off*) Not now, Papa. Au revoir, Papa.
Pochet Au revoir. Good-night, messieurs, dames!

Pochet exits

Palmyre (*to Amélie*) How brave of you to have changed jobs.
Amélie Not really. When I was a maid I learnt what the gentlemen wanted,
but they never paid me for it. An artist needs subsidy. Now I'm a cocotte
and I'm well paid.
Étienne (*off*) Damn it! Damn!

Yvonne (*to Amélie*) The voice of your subsidizer!
All Étienne!

Étienne enters in shirt-sleeves and the trousers of any army officer. He is carrying his tunic on his arm

Étienne Amélie! I am certain. Don't deny it. Absolutely certain.
Amélie Of what?
Étienne That I've grown. Look at my trousers!
Amélie Oh, I see!
Étienne (*pointing to his trousers which are two or three inches too short*) There's two inches more of me in here than the last time I was on parade.
Amélie I'm not complaining.
Bibichon (*to Amélie*) I'm sure you're not.
Étienne If I'd gone off to the barracks this evening like this I'd have looked very smart at the regimental parade! Can you lengthen them?
Amélie Yes, but you'd better try on the tunic while you're about it.
Étienne Right. Ouf! Those cigar fumes!
Bibichon If you bought better ones they wouldn't stink so much!
Amélie I'll have someone open the windows . . . (*She rings*)
Bibichon (*raising the collar of his jacket*) I don't want to catch my death of cold!
Étienne (*about his tunic*) Snug as a cannon's ball!
Bibichon The cold is bad for my digestion. (*He sits on the sofa again between Palmyre and Yvonne*) But if Yvonne hugs my back and Palmyre lies on my stomach . . .!

Bibichon squashes Yvonne against the sofa and pulls Palmyre on to his lap

Yvonne ⎱
Palmyre ⎰ (*together*) Get off!
Boas (*still playing cards*) You can do what you want with Palmyre but hands off Yvonne!
Bibichon I don't remember asking your opinion.
Boas Yvonne is *my* mistress.
Bibichon She may be your mistress but she can still be my mattress.
Yvonne Get off me! (*She aims a blow at his neck*)
Bibichon She's well-sprung too!
Yvonne Get off with you!
Bibichon (*to Boas*) Now I've made your bed you can lie in it!
Boas (*to Valcreuse*) He's insufferable!

Adonis enters. He is dressed as a footman, his livery decorated with golden buttons

Adonis You rang, madame?
Amélie Yes! Open the window. And then take away those cups and glasses that are lying around.
Adonis What a filthy mess.
Amélie Adonis!
Adonis Sorry sister mine.

Amélie Madame when you're on duty.
Adonis That's a nice way to speak to your brother!
Amélie You wouldn't have a job if you weren't my brother.
Bibichon Spare us the family quarrel, please!

The doorbell rings

   Adonis exits

Étienne Who would turn up at this hour? Are you expecting anyone?
Amélie No.
Yvonne (*offering to leave*) Listen, if you are expecting a . . .
Palmyre We'll leave.

   Adonis returns

Amélie Oh, please stay. You can wait through there. (*She points off*) I won't
be long. (*To Adonis*) Well, who is it?
Adonis A lady who wants to talk to you in private!
Étienne In private!
Amélie Who is she?
Adonis I don't know.
Amélie What do you mean, you don't know?
Adonis She wouldn't give me her name.
Amélie (*to everybody*) Always a bad sign! Does she look well-to-do?
Adonis (*pouting*) Pffut! (*Disdainfully*) Looks like a lady to me.
Étienne Don't you think much of ladies then?
Adonis Well, she hasn't got Amélie's style. She's dressed in very sombre
colours.
Bibichon Ah you like a bit of razzle-dazzle, do you?
Adonis You what?
Bibichon Pardon!
Amélie }
Pochet } (*together*) Manners, Adonis!
Adonis Sorry! It just slipped out.
Amélie She's probably collecting for charity. Ladies never come here for
anything else! (*To Adonis*) Ask her to come in.

   Adonis exits

Come on, Bibichon. You can take your drink with you.
Bibichon I like mysterious strangers.
Amélie Out.
Étienne We'll wait out here.

   All except Amélie leave the room

Bibichon (*to Boas*) Come on Boas!

   Adonis enters, showing in Irene

Adonis If Madame would come this way.
Amélie Come in please, madame.
Irene Do I have the pleasure of addressing Mademoiselle Amélie d'Avranches?

Amélie You do, madame.

Adonis exits

Irene Oh, mademoiselle, I'm approaching you on a subject of the greatest delicacy. I'm terribly nervous!

Amélie Calm yourself dear lady, I beg you.

Irene It's about a friend.

Amélie I see.

Irene (*eyeing her up for the first time*) But forgive me! Don't I know you from somewhere?

Amélie (*playing the lady*) Well, it is possible, madame. I'm frequently out in society.

Irene No, no. But . . . have you always been a . . . I mean, were you always a . . . er . . . a . . .

Amélie (*with self-importance*) Madame, I am the daughter of a former officer of the Republic.

Irene Oh, no, no then. Forgive me. It's just that you resemble somebody who . . .

Amélie I am not offended, madame. Now, where were we?

Irene Yes, I came about a friend. One of my closest friends. You will of course pardon me if I don't actually mention her by name?

Amélie Of course, madame.

Irene She's a married lady, you understand.

Amélie Have you come to talk to me about her husband?

Irene No, about her lover.

Amélie Oh!

Irene Mademoiselle, if you could only imagine how deeply she loves him!

Amélie Your friend?

Irene What? Oh, yes, my friend. This is her first lover, you see.

Amélie Poor thing!

Irene And you can't dream what the first lover means to a married woman. It opens up an exquisite world of delights, fights, nights and gentle pangs of conscience.

Amélie (*half smiling, half melancholy*) Oh, yes madame. Yes.

Irene (*in ecstasy*) The first delicious fall from grace!

Amélie Oh yes.

Irene Then you remember what it was like.

Amélie Yes, mine was a Great Dane.

Irene A dog?

Amélie No. My lover was from Denmark.

Irene Oh, I see. A Dane!

Amélie A Great Dane!

Irene Ah!

Amélie A lot of water has passed under the bridge since then.

Irene Not for my friend. This man is unique. If she were to lose him it would be too awful.

Amélie You really love him then?

Irene Madly!

Amélie You're very sweet.

Irene What? Oh mademoiselle. What have you made me say? It's not me. It's my friend.

Amélie Don't you trust me?

Irene Oh, mademoiselle!

Amélie Discretion is our professional duty.

Irene Oh well! What does it matter? One must act courageously. Yes, mademoiselle, it is I.

Amélie I had guessed.

Irene Mademoiselle, you can have all the men in the entire universe except him. Just let me keep him!

Amélie What are you talking about?

Irene Tell me it isn't true. Tell me he's not going to marry you.

Amélie What? Who?

Irene Marcel Courbois.

Amélie Marcel Courbois! And me! (*She bursts out laughing*) Ha, ha, ha! (*She gets up and walks towards the door*)

Irene Where are you going?

Amélie Just a moment! Étienne! Étienne!

Étienne (*off*) What?

Amélie Come here a minute!

Etienne enters

Étienne What is it?

Amélie (*unable to speak for laughing*) It's Madame, here! Ha, ha, ha!

Étienne Madame.

Amélie She came to tell me——

Irene Her close friend . . .

Amélie —wanted to know if I was going to marry Marcel Courbois.

Étienne Aha!

Amélie Madame's lov . . . friend . . .

Étienne Marcel Courbois . . . and you . . . I've never heard anything so . . .

They both double up with laughter

Irene I'm so pleased you find the whole thing so ridiculous!

Amélie }
Étienne } (*together*) Ridiculous.

Irene You don't know how happy you've made me.

Étienne You mean how happy we've made your friend!

Irene Pardon? Oh yes, of course, my friend!

Amélie I'm afraid, chérie, you're not fooling anybody.

Irene I'd better make a clean breast of it then.

Étienne What on earth made you think that about Marcel Courbois?

Irene Walking to church this morning . . .

Étienne Yes . . .?

Irene I had to pass his house.

Étienne I understand completely.

Irene Certainly, fortune favours the brave. Anyway, while he was putting his clothes on——

Étienne Again!

Irene No, no. He was in bed when I arrived.

Étienne Oh!

Irene I happened to flick through some papers on his desk.

Étienne Perfectly natural.

Irene And I found a letter. It was a rough draft of something Marcel had written to his godfather in Holland telling him about his forthcoming marriage to Mademoiselle Amélie d'Avranches.

Amélie To me!

Irene What does it mean?

Amélie I don't know!

Étienne Didn't you ask Marcel?

Irene How could I? What if it had been true? The shame! The disgrace! And my humiliation at revealing how I had discovered his appalling secret!

Amélie So you preferred to come to me instead.

Irene Yes!

Étienne I can't answer the riddle for you, but as soon as I see Marcel I'll ask him. He's one of my best friends.

Irene Ah!

Étienne He confides in me like a brother! So the fact that Amélie is *my* mistress should be enough to satisfy you of——

Irene He confides in you?

Étienne Everything.

Irene Then, you must know about me?

Étienne Of course, Madame la Comtesse!

Amélie (*suddenly realizing*) The Countess! Of course. I knew that voice straight away! I recognized that tone of command. Aren't you the Countess of Premilly?

Irene Do you know me then? (*She lifts her veil*)

Amélie Of course I do. Don't you know who I am?

Irene (*looking through her lorgnette*) Is it Amélie?

Amélie Amélie Pochet, at your service!

Irene My old chambermaid!

Amélie The same.

Irene My dear child!

Étienne You were her chambermaid!

Amélie Damn! I'd forgotten you were here! Sorry madame!

Irene For what?

Amélie I said "Damn"!

Irene But can it really be you! This house, your changed circumstances! This luxurious apartment. And your hair has changed colour.

Amélie Yes, it's got lighter. I don't know why!

Irene You left me as a Pochet and now you've become a d'Avranches.

Amélie Well Pochet wasn't very good for business. And is Madame keeping well? And Monsieur?

Irene Monsieur is fine, thank you, Amélie. He's not been well, poor man.

Amélie Good. Good.

Irene Come and sit down my dear.

Amélie In Madame's company?

Irene Please!

Amélie (*sitting*) It's a great honour.

Irene Amélie, I'm so relieved that such a sordid affair could turn into such a pleasant occasion. Imagine me stepping into a world that I'm entirely ignorant of . . . and finding that I'm already acquainted with its inhabitants!

Amélie Yes!

Irene (*with sympathy*) And so, you've become a . . .

Amélie A cocotte. Yes Madame la Comtesse.

Irene But how did you fall into such a . . .

Amélie Ambition, madame. I wasn't cut out to be a chambermaid.

Irene That's a pity. You were good at your job.

Étienne She still is!

Amélie Étienne!

Irene Well, you always were a coquette. You liked wearing cheap jewellery and garters?

Amélie Yes.

Irene And dousing yourself in perfume?

Amélie Yes.

Irene Mine!

Amélie On my wages I had no alternative.

Irene You used to borrow my dresses without telling me!

Amélie But I always put them back.

Irene You always wanted to look like the ladies. (*Touching her hair*) That's why you had to leave us.

Étienne Why?

Amélie (*to Étienne*) She didn't like the competition.

Étienne Ah!

Irene Still, I'm very sorry you had to go.

Amélie Madame, you're very kind.

Irene It's so difficult to get a good chambermaid nowadays.

Amélie You don't need to tell me. The concept of service doesn't seem to exist any more.

Irene (*lowering her veil*) There are people waiting for you.

Amélie For me?

Yvonne (*off*) It's us.

Amélie Madame, forgive me. Would you mind?

Irene Not at all. Not at all.

Étienne (*to Irene*) Excuse us, madame.

The others enter on their way to the front door

Amélie What is it?

Palmyre We're off.

Boas Yes, goodbye.

Valcreuse Goodbye.

Étienne You're all going.

Bibichon We're queuing to get out. Like the English.

Amélie Good-night then. I'm sorry not to be able to show you all out. Do the honours, Papa.

Étienne I'll see you all soon. In twenty-eight days time when I get back from Rouen.

All In twenty-eight days then.

Pochet Of course!

All Goodbye, goodbye.

Amélie Bye! Goodbye.

Étienne Goodbye, goodbye.

The others exit

Amélie Madame la Comtesse, I can't tell you how happy I am. I was so devoted to you.

Étienne Why is it that as soon as servants leave your service they become devoted to you?

Amélie (*reproachfully*) Étienne!

Irene How true! (*To Étienne*) Monsieur, if you're Marcel's best friend then you must be M. Étienne de Milledieu.

Étienne Oh, he's talked to you about me then?

Irene And said some very nice things too. (*Peering at him*) Only he didn't tell me . . .(*Looking at his uniform*) . . . You've chosen a fine career.

Étienne Some people think so.

Irene What are you?

Étienne A broker . . . at the Stock Exchange.

Irene I didn't know they wore uniforms.

Étienne They don't. Not yet anyway. This is for my twenty-eight days' call up.

Pochet enters

Pochet There I've cleared the jam. (*Seeing Irene*) Oh, excuse me!

Amélie No, stay! (*Introducing him*) Papa.

Pochet Madame.

Irene I remember him perfectly!

Amélie Don't you recognize Madame? Madame la Comtesse de Premilly!

Pochet (*changing tone completely and making small salutes*) Good heavens! So it is, so it is!

Irene You often used to come to my house to visit your daughter. Don't you remember? You were a policeman then.

Pochet Brigadier. If I remember rightly . . . And is life treating you well? (*He offers her his hand*)

Irene (*not taking it*) Very well, thank you.

Pochet We're none of us getting any younger.

Irene What?

Amélie Papa!

Étienne You're full of compliments.

Pochet Oh no, madame. I meant no offence. I didn't mean that I thought Madame had aged. She's matured, ripened . . . a lot . . .
Amélie She's not a Camembert, Papa!

There is a ring at the door

Irene Amélie, I must leave you.
Amélie You're going, madame?
Irene You've got company.

Adonis enters

Adonis It's Monsieur Courbois.
Irene Marcel!

Marcel enters

Marcel Bonjour mes enfants! (*Bumping into Irene*) Irene!

Adonis exits

Irene My darling, I——
Marcel What the hell are you doing here? (*He changes tone*) Madame!
Étienne "Madame"!
Marcel You don't belong in this place!
Amélie Hey!
Marcel She doesn't.
Irene My dearest I can explain everything.
Étienne Wait a moment. You've got the explaining to do. What about all these stories about marrying Amélie?
Marcel What?
Pochet Are you going to marry my daughter?
Marcel Of course not. Who told you that?
Irene Forgive me. It was me.
Marcel But how did you know?
Irene From a letter I read . . .
Marcel What!
Étienne (*ironically*) By mistake.
Marcel You were going through my letters, madame?
Étienne Pretend we're not here. Call her what you like!
Marcel You doubted me!
Irene I did!
Amélie What's it all about, Marcel?
Marcel All right, I'll tell you. I'm in terrible trouble. Our marriage is the only way out.
Irene You *are* going to marry her then?
Marcel Of course not. I was only going to pretend to.
All Pretend?
Irene Why?
Marcel Because I'm fed up being flat broke.
Irene Oh!
Marcel I haven't got a sou.

Irene My poor lamb! Is that really true? But I could——

Marcel That's enough! I still have some pride.

Amélie You're so old-fashioned.

Irene (*to Amélie*) Quite so!

Marcel It's ridiculous. There am I with a fortune of one million francs——

Irene A million francs?

Amélie A million!

Pochet A mill——

Marcel Yes. One million francs.

Pochet (*sitting him down forcibly*) Won't you sit down my dear young man?

Étienne You're wasting your time. He can't touch it.

Pochet (*standing him up forcibly*) What do you mean?

Marcel My poor father couldn't believe that a young man could manage such a fortune without wasting it on cocottes.

Amélie Charming!

Marcel And so he left just enough to keep the wolf from the door; an allowance of a thousand francs! I'm on my uppers!

Amélie Appalling!

Pochet But that's more than I got when I was with the police.

All Shhhhhh!!

Marcel Meanwhile he gave the million francs in trust to my godfather in Holland, and charged him to hand it over to me on my wedding day.

Irene Your wedding day! Now I understand.

Marcel Desperate measures. My fortune is at risk.

Étienne And so you told your godfather you were going to marry Amélie.

Marcel Precisely.

Étienne (*cynically*) She's a very nice girl!

Marcel Well of course she is. Mademoiselle Amélie d'Avranches is a young lady from an excellent family!

Pochet Daughter of an old Police Superin——

Amélie coughs

—argeant.

Marcel I sent him her photograph. I didn't have anyone else's photo handy.

Amélie You're such a sweet boy! And now my photograph's somewhere in Holland.

Pochet Like a dyke!

Étienne Well, mon vieux. You seem to have got it all worked out.

Marcel But I haven't. That's just it. It won't work at all. That's why I'm here.

All Why?

Marcel My godfather wasn't satisfied with what I said in the letter and he decided to come and see for himself. He's just arrived in Paris. "Ach mein klein godsonny"—he lives in Holland but he was born in Rotenburg. "Ach mein klein godsonny zis is a surprise, ja?"

Étienne Lovely!

Marcel You're telling me. "I wish to the pure young lady introduced to be."

Amélie (*laughing*) And I'm the pure young lady, am I?

Étienne (*laughing also*) Yes, you're the pure young lady!

Pochet Why are you laughing? She isn't married as far as I know.

Étienne (*put out and turning away*) Technically correct!

Marcel Étienne, please don't be like that! Amélie, please! You won't leave me in the lurch, will you?

Amélie I certainly will.

Marcel A million francs! You won't make me lose that?

Irene Amélie, my dear. You can't make him lose that!

Amélie Well . . .

Pochet No you can't, you can't!

Marcel (*grasping Amélie's hands*) Try to imagine one million francs. Think what a nice present I'll give you.

Amélie I don't want your presents.

Pochet You do! You can't say things like that. It's impolite.

Amélie I suppose it is. (*To Pochet*) Well I'll do it for your sake. And then there's Madame . . . to whom I am deeply devoted.

Marcel (*looking surprised at Irene*) Madame!

Irene She and I share a secret.

Marcel Well Amélie?

Amélie I'll do my best.

Marcel Thank you Amélie. (*He shakes her hand*)

Irene (*shaking Amélie's hand*) Thank you dear Amélie.

Étienne What about the wedding? Won't he notice there isn't a wedding?

All Of course!

Marcel It's all right. He's leaving for a two month stay in America so I've fixed the wedding date while he's away. He said to me "Listen, klein godsonny"—although he lives in Holland——

All He was born in Rotenburg.

Marcel Have I already told you?

All Yes.

Marcel "Listen, klein godsonny. For the ceremony I am not there, but the money certainly."

Amélie (*tendering her hand*) My fiancé, here is my hand.

Marcel (*with comic zeal*) Ah! Mademoiselle!

Pochet (*embracing him*) My son-in-law!

Marcel Father-in-law, you're all I could have wished for!

Étienne And when is your godfather coming?

Marcel I don't know! Today! Sometime! Now even!

The doorbell rings

There he is!

Irene I must slip away.

Amélie But why are you going, madame?

Irene What part would I play in this family gathering?

Adonis appears at the hall door

Marcel (*to Adonis*) Well? Is it my godfather?

Adonis General Koshnadieff!

All What!

Amélie Who is Koshnadieff?
Adonis I've no idea.
Amélie Well, go and ask him then.
Adonis All right.

Adonis exits

Irene (*taking her leave*) Dear Amélie.
Amélie My dear Madame la Comtesse. You don't know how happy you've made me.
Irene You're a dear, dear girl.
Amélie If ever Madame has need of me . . . or of my father . . .
Pochet At your service.
Irene Thank you, Amélie. Thank you, Pochet.

Adonis enters

Adonis He says he's come on a diplomatic mission.
Amélie What does he mean "diplomatic mission"?
Étienne Ask him to come in and you'll find out.
Amélie Tell him to come in. I'll be with him in a minute.

Adonis exits

Étienne (*to Marcel*) I'm going to get out of my uniform. Are you coming Marcel?
Marcel Fine. (*To Irene*) Au revoir darling, 'til later.
Irene Au revoir Marcel. Goodbye Amélie.
Amélie We'll show you to the door.
Pochet Of course!
Irene (*to Étienne*) Monsieur.
Étienne Delighted, madame. (*To Marcel*) Come on you!

Marcel and Étienne exit R

Amélie This way, Madame la Comtesse.

Pochet, Amélie and Irene exit through the alcove

Adonis shows Koshnadieff into the room

Adonis If Monsieur would just step this way.

Koshnadieff is dressed in uniform. He has a strong Slav accent. He looks about the room appreciatively

Koshnadieff Charming. Just a minute . . .
Adonis Monsieur?
Koshnadieff Where is the lady of the house?
Adonis She'll be here directly.
Koshnadieff Good, good.

As Adonis makes to leave

Valet.

Adonis Yes, monsieur.
Koshnadieff What's she like? Many lovers? One? Half a dozen?
Adonis Who?
Koshnadieff The mistress of the house.
Adonis I don't know, monsieur. You'll have to ask her yourself.
Koshnadieff Stupid man! That's all. Dismissed.
Adonis (*aside*) Foreigner! (*He makes to leave*)
Koshnadieff Valet, take this Louis.
Adonis Oh thank you, monsieur. (*He makes to go again*)
Koshnadieff And bring me some small change.
Adonis (*disappointedly*) Oh?
Koshnadieff Yes.
Adonis Is that all?
Koshnadieff That's all.
Adonis (*aside*) Kossack. (*Seeing Amélie off*) Here is Madame.

Adonis exits

Amélie enters

Amélie Monsieur?
Koshnadieff General Koshnadieff. At your service. First aide-de-camp of his Royal Highness Prince Nicholas of Palestrie.
Amélie I am most honoured, general, but——
Koshnadieff I have been sent to your side by his Highness.
Amélie His Highness?
Koshnadieff The Prince is in love with you.
Amélie With me? He has never met me.
Koshnadieff I beg your pardon. Didn't you go to the gala when the Prince made his last official visit to Paris? Weren't you sitting in the orchestra stalls?
Amélie Yes, but——
Koshnadieff His Highness saw you there.
Amélie (*flattered*) Really?
Koshnadieff He even asked the President of the Republic who you were.
Amélie No!
Koshnadieff But the President couldn't tell him.
Amélie Ah?
Koshnadieff No.
Amélie How surprising.
Koshnadieff And so an embassy attaché got in touch with the local police and yesterday they sent us your file.
Amélie My file!
Koshnadieff A dossier. From which the Prince was able to find out who you were.
Amélie (*easily but vexed*) Very gallant.
Koshnadieff Oh his Highness is very smitten! He is hooked . . . as you say. (*Confidentially*) If he were to come here incognito it would be to your advantage.
Amélie Here?

Koshnadieff His Highness arrived in Paris this morning to visit the President, but the very first thing the Prince said to me when he got to the hotel, was how much he cares for you. "Koshnadieff, my good man," he said, "Run to her and arrange things for me. I'm counting on you."

Amélie Well, well!

Koshnadieff So here I am to prepare the way, as we say, for the big push.

Amélie (*taken aback*) So you've come to . . .

Koshnadieff I know it's a delicate matter. Perhaps you aren't used to this kind of approach.

Amélie It's not that. It happens every day. But it's not usually a general who does it.

Koshnadieff Really?

Amélie No.

Koshnadieff (*proudly*) In Palestrie, it's I who have the honour of undertaking such responsibilities. I am after all, his Highness's aide-de-camp.

Amélie Of course, of course!

Koshnadieff Now, tell me. When?

Amélie When!

Koshnadieff Which night would you prefer?

Amélie I like your style. But I am afraid I'm not free, General. I already have a lover!

Koshnadieff So? What does that matter? Perhaps he'd like a medal? Commander of our Order.

Amélie Monsieur, I am faithful to him.

Koshnadieff Knight of the Garter, then? With an insignia of his own?

Amélie You don't understand!

Koshnadieff (*scandalized*) You're surely not refusing? You're not going to turn his Highness down?

Amélie I didn't say that.

Koshnadieff Well what's stopping you then?

Amélie (*hesitating*) Well . . . well . . .

Koshnadieff (*whispering the words like the devil himself*) Think what it's like to have a Royal Highness in your bed! To deceive your lover with a Royal Highness isn't really like deceiving him at all.

Amélie Particularly if one isn't obliged to tell him.

Koshnadieff God in heaven, no.

Amélie In fact my lover is just about to leave for his military service in Rouen.

Koshnadieff You see how the Lord orders our lives.

Amélie A Royal Highness!

Koshnadieff The Prince is very generous.

Amélie Oh my lover gives me everything I need.

Koshnadieff I don't doubt it. But besides everything you need . . .

Amélie There's all those things one wants.

Koshnadieff Many, many things.

Amélie Many, many.

Koshnadieff Well?

Amélie Well . . .

Koshnadieff Agreed then. (*He pats her bottom*) One more thing. It's his Highness's custom to make a donation of ten thousand francs after each visit.

Amélie Ten thousand francs!

Koshnadieff Ten thousand.

Amélie (*whistling*) Phew!

Koshnadieff So I will let you have nine thousand. Agreed?

Amélie Nine thousand?

Koshnadieff Nine.

Amélie (*realizing*) Oh, because you . . .

Koshnadieff (*looking at her disdainfully*) Hem!

Amélie Yes that's fine. Nine. Nine thousand.

Koshnadieff Agreed then.

Amélie (*aside*) Lovely fellow!

Pochet enters

Pochet Excuse me. Here's the change you asked for.

Amélie What?

Koshnadieff Ah, yes. Thank you. Keep this for your trouble. *(He gives him one of the twenty sous coins)*

Pochet Thanks.

Amélie Father. May I present, General . . . I'm sorry.

Koshnadieff Koshnadieff!

Amélie First aide-de-camp of the Prince of Palestrie.

Pochet Phew!

Koshnadieff Pleased to meet you.

Pochet thinks the General wants to shake his hand but he doesn't and Pochet rather philosophically puts it back in his pocket

Very pleased! Perhaps you'd like to be a Commander of the Order of Palestrie?

Pochet What me? Well, yes, of course I would. But why?

Koshnadieff For exceptional services. His Highness has the hots for your daughter.

Pochet (*biting his lips*) I see.

Koshnadieff He sent me to make the first move.

Pochet Pardon me but is this a request for her hand?

Koshnadieff All the parts.

Pochet Then I beg you not to go any further in front of me.

Koshnadieff I don't understand.

Pochet (*with dignity*) I am her father.

Koshnadieff Of course. (*Pointing to Amélie*) It's just between us then. Very shortly I shall have the honour to conduct his Highness to your home.

Pochet What here? The Prince here?

Koshnadieff Absolutely.

Pochet (*as if the Prince were there*) Please take a seat.

Koshnadieff Thank you.

Pochet Not you. I'm talking to the Prince. Oh my God, my God. And I'm not properly dressed. And the flags aren't out.
Koshnadieff I beg you, calm yourself. No fuss! The Prince likes his anonymity.
Pochet What a pity. It would have impressed the neighbours.

Marcel enters hurriedly

Marcel Amélie, Amélie. (*To Koshnadieff*) Oh! Forgive me, monsieur.
Koshnadieff Not at all!
Marcel He's here! He's here! I've just seen him through the window!
Amélie Who?
Marcel My godfather! Van Putzeboum!
Pochet (*laughing at the name*) What?
Marcel (*laughing*) That's his name. He was born with it.
Pochet Putzeboum!
Marcel Van! Van!

There is a ring at the doorbell

That's him.
Amélie Aren't you going to show him in?

Marcel goes into the hall

Through the hall window we see Adonis letting in Van Putzeboum who kisses Marcel

Koshnadieff Madame. I must take my leave.
Amélie Goodbye, General. I look forward to your next visit.
Koshnadieff So do I. (*To Pochet*) Goodbye, monsieur.
Pochet (*bowing*) General. You won't forget my little medal, will you?
Koshnadieff Of course not. (*He starts to exit*)
Pochet When I say "little", that's not to say I'd refuse a big one.

Amélie, Koshnadieff and Pochet exit as . . .

Marcel and Van Putzeboum enter

Marcel This way, Godfather.
Van Putzeboum (*he speaks with a pronounced German accent*) Vell. Here are you mine little godsonny. And here am I, also! On the dot. Here in the fine bosom of your new family, I am correct? (*He puts his hat on the card table*)
Marcel Yes, of course, Godfather.

Amélie enters with Pochet

Van Putzeboum (*looking at Amélie with satisfaction*) Ah! Goodbye!
Marcel Godfather, may I introduce you to——
Van Putzeboum Wait, wait my little godsonny, let me guess. Mademoiselle Amélie d'Avranches, I am correct?
Amélie That's me.
Van Putzeboum I am correct!
Pochet (*aside*) Brilliant!

Amélie (*remembering her social graces*) Monsieur Marcel told us of your impending arrival, monsieur, and we were looking forward to it with impatience.

Van Putzeboum (*flattered*) Good! Good!

Amélie (*to Pochet*) Isn't that so, Papa?

Pochet Like the racing results.

Van Putzeboum You are so very kind. Gottverdeck, little godsonny, I congratulate you! She's a fine-looking ladle.

Amélie Monsieur!

Van Putzeboum Yes, yes. I always say what is correct!

Marcel You do?

Van Putzeboum Of course I do! (*To Pochet*) Am I correct, monsieur?

Pochet You are talking about my daughter!

Van Putzeboum Oyoyoyoy! Really? Do I address Monsieur d'Avranches?

Pochet Pochet.

Amélie and Marcel signal to Pochet

Amélie Hem!

Pochet Pochet . . . d'Avranches! Pochet d'Avranches at your service.

Van Putzeboum I'm delightful. (*Tendering his hand*) Your hand, monsieur. Goodbye. (*To Amélie*) Mademoiselle, what you wish I wish.

Amélie My dear godfather!

Van Putzeboum That's correct. You must call me Godvater. It helps to shorten the miles between us. (*He makes to kiss her. To Marcel*) Do you mind if I give her a smack?

Marcel What?

Van Putzeboum A smack. You know a smack? You know what a smack is?

Marcel Oh yes! Smack her, smack her.

Van Putzeboum (*to Amélie*) Can I smack you?

Amélie Well I . . .

Marcel He means may he kiss you?

Amélie Oh! Of course you may.

Van Putzeboum (*kissing her*) What a cheeky virgin! (*He kisses the other cheek. To Pochet*) Like kissing a baby's where it comes out. Now Mademoiselle Amélie, are you pleased to be marrying my klein godsonny.

Amélie Yes, I love the klein godsonny. I mean I love Monsieur Marcel and I am very happy to become his wife.

Van Putzeboum Did you hear that, little godsonny?

Marcel (*embracing Amélie*) I'd give my life for those sweet words of love!

Amélie (*pushing him away*) Not before our nuptials dearest!

Marcel Forgive me.

Van Putzeboum What a chaste young ladle! She's as pure as gold!

Marcel And that's a rarity these days.

Pochet What, gold?

Marcel No, chastity!

Pochet Gold's pretty hard to come by too!

Van Putzeboum Now if you'll allow me, I have brought you something. Please accept this little gift. I am mounting you especially.

Amélie For me. (*Looking at the ring which Van Putzeboum has given her*) What a sparkler!

Van Putzeboum But it's a diamond!

Amélie Yes, of course. Sparkler is a modern expression for beautiful . . . fine. How fine it is!

Van Putzeboum (*repeating*) A shparkler, yes, a shparkler!

Amélie And you're very fine too. Let me give you a kiss.

Van Putzeboum (*pulling away*) You are very playful ja?

Amélie Look, Papa! Marcel!

Marcel Superb!

Pochet Magnificent!

Van Putzeboum Not bad at all. It's a shparkler.

All (*laughing*) A shparkler.

Van Putzeboum Shparklers are my speciality.

Amélie ⎫
Pochet ⎭ (*together*) Oh?

Van Putzeboum Yes, in Holland I tread in diamonds.

Pochet (*inspecting Van Putzeboum's feet*) What an occupation!

Van Putzeboum And though I say it myself, that diamond is worthy of a collection.

Pochet All we've got to do is get the set!

Van Putzeboum Yes, but now it's up to her husband. Isn't that so little godsonny.

Marcel What do you mean?

Van Putzeboum Now that you're going to get your hands on the fortune.

Marcel When?

Van Putzeboum As soon as you've been to the Town Hall.

Marcel The Town Hall.

Van Putzeboum To the Burgomeister! Your wedding!

Marcel Oh that! (*Aside*) Damn!

Amélie (*making the ring sparkle in the light*) Isn't it pretty? (*To Van Putzeboum*) I must give you another kiss!

Van Putzeboum Come on then, my dear. Don't be embarrassed. Am I correct in thinking I've made you happy?

Amélie I certainly like diamonds better than flowers.

Van Putzeboum Ah! Did you get my bucket?

Amélie Bucket? No. Have you seen a bucket, Father?

Pochet I haven't seen any bucket.

Van Putzeboum Nobody brought you my bucket of flowers? Well, wouldn't you know it? Who do those idiots think they are? Do you have a telephone handy so I can give them a good telling off?

Amélie Yes of course we have.

Van Putzeboum It was the florist in the Boulevard de la Madeleine, the one that sells wedding buckets and funerary tributes.

Marcel Landozel!

Van Putzeboum That's it! I think. They are stupid in that shop. I told them, "It's for Mademoiselle Amélie d'Avranches, the young ladle who is going to marry Monsieur Courbois; you must know her." "No. We only know the Amélie d'Avranches who knocks around with Monsieur de Milledieu."

All (*aside and various*) God! No! Heavens! *etc.*

Van Putzeboum "That isn't it at all", I said, "Mademoiselle d'Avranches is a lady of the highest breeding who is engaged to marry Marcel Courbois." Imagine, they thought you were a cocotte. (*Realizing that he is facing Amélie*) Oh forgive me! That I should say such things to your front!

Amélie I didn't understand a word, monsieur.

Van Putzeboum What an innocent! Your husband can explain it all later! Can't you little godsonny?

Marcel (*to Amélie*) Yes, it's not really meant for the ears of young ladles.

Amélie That's all right my dear. I really don't want to know.

Étienne enters

Étienne Here I am. Changed!

All Oh!

Marcel (*aside*) Oops!

Marcel seizes Van Putzeboum

Van Putzeboum What is it? What's the matter?

Marcel Monsieur . . . Monsieur . . .

Amélie Monsieur . . . Chopart.

Marcel Paul, Paul Chopart.

Étienne What?

Marcel (*aside*) Shut up.

Amélie My cousin!

Marcel Her cousin?

Pochet Amélie's cousin.

Van Putzeboum Really? Well, well, well.

Étienne (*aside*) Her cousin?

Van Putzeboum Monsieur, my compliments.

Étienne Pleased to meet you. (*Aside, annoyed*) Her cousin!

Pochet This is Monsieur Van Badeboum.

Van Putzeboum Putzeboum. I am a Putz!

Pochet Putzeboum, that's it. Putzeboum.

Étienne Delighted!

Van Putzeboum Goodbye. I knew a Chopart in Rotenburg.

Étienne How nice for you!

Van Putzeboum Chopart, yes. He was in aniseed balls.

Étienne How sweet for him!

Van Putzeboum No relation, I suppose?

Étienne I have no relations with aniseed balls.

Van Putzeboum Pity. Good business, aniseed balls. I recommend them to you.

Étienne Thanks!

Van Putzeboum (*to the others*) Now, if you'll forgive me, I'll go and talk to the flowers.

Amélie Of course. (*To Pochet*) Will you lead the way, Papa. The telephone is in my bedroom.

Pochet This way, please.

Van Putzeboum (*leaving behind Pochet*) I will give a section of my mind to this florist, with his Monsieur de Milledieu!

Étienne What's going on?

Marcel restrains Étienne

Van Putzeboum This makes me laugh. Monsieur Milledieu!

Étienne He's laughing at me.

Marcel (*restraining Étienne*) Calm down.

Van Putzeboum What a fool! Hallo!

Van Putzeboum and Pochet exit

Étienne Explain!

Marcel Be quiet.

Étienne How dare he call me a fool!

Marcel He wasn't calling you a fool.

Étienne What?

Marcel It was the florist.

Étienne What florist?

Marcel The one he ordered the bucket from.

Étienne What bucket.

Marcel The bucket for Amélie.

Amélie Don't you understand anything, Étienne?

Étienne Not one word.

Amélie The florist told him the only Mademoiselle d'Avranches he knew was the one with Monsieur de Milledieu.

Étienne So?

Amélie So now you understand why I couldn't introduce you?

Étienne Why not?

Amélie Because Marcel Courbois' fiancée couldn't very well be Monsieur de Milledieu's mistress.

Étienne That's why I've become Chopart!

Amélie }
Marcel } (*together*) Exactly!

Étienne (*disgruntled*) I'm glad you're enjoying yourselves.

Marcel It'll only be for a few days, Étienne. Once he's gone you can have your name back.

Étienne How very kind of you.

Pochet enters

Pochet Will you come a moment, Amélie? We can't get through.

Amélie I'm coming. (*To Étienne*) Oh! let me show you the beautiful ring he's given me.

Étienne (*sullenly*) Great.

Amélie Just look at it.

Pochet Please hurry!

Amélie (*pretending to go*) I'm coming. (*Putting the ring under Étienne's nose*) Pretty, eh?

Étienne Very pretty!

Pochet (*dragging Amélie off*) Are you coming?

Amélie (*trailing her arm behind her and waving her ring finger*) Pretty, isn't it? Really pretty.

She and Pochet exit

Étienne Yes! Yes! Yes!

Marcel Listen, mon vieux. I'm really sorry to drag you into all this.

Étienne It doesn't matter. Why should I worry? I'm just about to leave anyway.

Marcel I'm glad you feel like that.

Étienne Besides it gives me the opportunity to ask you a favour.

Marcel Go on.

Étienne Well, you know how crazy I am about Amélie. I'd like to have taken her with me but then I thought . . . a garrison town, lots of superior officers . . . and when you have a pretty mistress in tow . . . you can't be too careful!

Marcel But Amélie's faithful to the core.

Étienne Oh I don't think otherwise! Until it's proved to the contrary! On the other hand, leaving her in Paris on her own, she's bound to get bored. She's got plenty of friends, of course, but actually, deep down I don't trust one of them. They're all swine!

Marcel Swine?

Étienne There's really only you. You're my best friend. I trust you like I trust myself. Amélie's very fond of you, so please, while I'm away I'm putting her in your care. Keep an eye on Amélie.

Marcel An eye?

Étienne Yes take her out. To the theatre, to lunch, dinner, supper, get her going.

Marcel Even that?

Étienne Yes! No, I didn't mean . . . it's an expression! It means, keep her occupied, dinners, suppers . . .

Marcel (*laughing*) Great!

Étienne Not to enjoy yourself, but to stop her from having these little evening soirées when things . . .

Marcel I understand perfectly. You can trust me!

Étienne I know I can.

They shake on it

Marcel Don't worry. I'll keep an eye on Amélie.

They utter their war cry

Étienne Hon.

Marcel Hon, hon.

Étienne Hon! Hon! Hon!

Van Putzeboum enters followed by Amélie

Van Putzeboum Goodbye, it isn't correct. I go there myself. Hallo.

Amélie No, no, Godfather.

Van Putzeboum Yes, I assure you. Will you come with me little godsonny?

Marcel Where?

Van Putzeboum To the florists. I have a taxiderm waiting downstairs.

Marcel A what?
Van Putzeboum A taxiderm.
Marcel Oh a taxiderm! Yes, yes!
Van Putzeboum We'll be back as soon as we leave!
Marcel Yes.
Van Putzeboum Are you coming?
Marcel Willingly.

Pochet enters

Pochet We couldn't get connected.
Van Putzeboum I kept getting crossed lines to little people who I said "Get off" to. Then somebody wanted to talk to Monsieur de Milledieu!
Étienne To me?
Van Putzeboum No, to Milledieu! As though he lived here!
Étienne But who wanted to talk to Monsieur de Milledieu?
Van Putzeboum How should I know? Do you think I asked? I'm fed up with this Millidieu person.
Étienne What?
Amélie Yes, we're all fed up with him. Sick to death!
Van Putzeboum Until later, eh? Hallo!
Amélie Till later. See them out, Papa.

All exit except Amélie and Étienne

Étienne Now he's cutting me off from the outside world. I'm furious. I resent him insulting my friends. Imbecile!
Amélie You're going away in less than a quarter of an hour and all you can think about is the telephone instead of dedicating these last few minutes to your Amélie!
Étienne You're right. We haven't been alone together since this morning.
Amélie You've noticed at last.
Étienne Well . . .
Amélie Well . . .
Étienne For the next twenty-eight days I shall be leading a life of abstinence.
Amélie My little monk!
Étienne When two people part for such a long time do they just shake hands?
Amélie Oh no!
Étienne Perhaps they say a last little goodbye?
Amélie They should.
Étienne Privately!
Amélie Of course.
Étienne Your bedroom looks very pretty.
Amélie (*pretending to be prim*) Now, now.
Étienne Come and see how pretty it is.
Amélie Oh, Étienne, Étienne!
Étienne (*dragging her*) Come and see. It's very pretty!
Amélie You're such a brute!

Pochet enters

Pochet Where are you two going?
Étienne Nowhere! We were just going to use the telephone.

There is a ring at the door

Amélie Te—le—phone!

Amélie and Étienne exit to the bedroom

Pochet I don't know why they bother! You can never get through!

Adonis enters

Adonis This way! This way!
Pochet Who is it?
Adonis (*pushing back the furniture*) Flowers! And what beauties! Come in, men!

Van Putzeboum enters followed by Marcel and two Florist's Boys

Van Putzeboum Come in and watch you don't damage them.

The two Florists carrying each side of a huge bouquet place it on the card table

Pochet My goodness!
Van Putzeboum Now fancy that! We were just on our way out when we bumped into the bucket that these two were delivering!
Pochet Fancy!

The doorbell rings

Adonis Someone's at the door.

Adonis exits

Van Putzeboum (*to the Florist's Boys*) Put it there will you? But where is the financée for whom they're intended?

The Florist's Boys exit

Pochet She's in her bedroom. On the telephone.
Van Putzeboum Oh the telephone. Yes.

Adonis enters

Adonis Oh my God, you'll never guess . . .
Pochet Who is it?
Adonis The Prince. The Prince of Palestrie!
Pochet My God. And you left him out there in the hall!
Adonis No, he's coming up!
Pochet Now line up, both of you! Line up!
Van Putzeboum } (*together*) What for?
Marcel
Pochet The King! It's the King! You hide behind the shrubbery! Music. We must have music. My God! Get the candelabra out! (*To Adonis*) Candles! Light the candles!

A record is put on the gramophone

Adonis But why?

Pochet Because . . . the King will expect it. (*To Van Putzeboum and Marcel*) Don't huddle. Spread out. Give him air. Keep moving. Keep moving . . .

Van Putzeboum (*enraged*) One moment, I insist!

Music begins to play

The Prince and Koshnadieff enter

Pochet Sire!

Prince (*turning to Koshnadieff*) So many people! Ah, the national anthem. (*He takes off his cloak*)

All remain with heads inclined

Koshnadieff May I introduce to your Highness the father of Mademoiselle d'Avranches.

Prince Ah very good! I compliment you . . . Commander of the Order.

Pochet (*kneeling, taking the Prince's hand and kissing it*) Oh, sire!

Prince (*commenting on the candle Pochet is holding under his nose*) But what's this? Were you just off to bed?

Pochet No, sire! It is for you.

Prince I wouldn't know what to do with it. And your delightful daughter isn't here?

Pochet She will be sire! In the meantime perhaps I can find you a substitute.

Prince Quite definitely not!

Pochet I'll go and get her, sire! Amélie!

Amélie
Étienne } (*together; off*) Don't come in. Leave us alone!

Pochet Oh my God! (*To Koshnadieff and the Prince*) This way, your Highness! This way, my Prince!

He starts to exit backwards with his candle in his hand, backs into Van Putzeboum, Adonis, Marcel, starts pushing them about as if he were directing traffic

Move, move. Don't stop still. Move, move! (*He looks back to the Prince*) This way, your Highness, this way. (*He doesn't know which way to go*)

Amélie
Étienne } (*together; off, in the height of ecstasy*) Ohhhh!

All look towards their bedroom

CURTAIN

ACT II

Marcel Courbois' bedroom

As the Curtain *rises the room is in almost total darkness. Only the night-light above the bed illuminates the room dimly*

The hall door opens and Charlotte enters bringing in breakfast on a tray

Charlotte Monsieur! Monsieur!
Marcel Hoooah.
Charlotte Monsieur!

Pause

Marcel (*yawning*) What time is it?
Charlotte (*shouting*) It's half-past twelve.
Marcel So what!
Charlotte (*shrugging her shoulders in agreement*) Ouf! I brought your chocolate. (*Beat*) Cho—co—late.
Marcel Choc-o-what?
Charlotte Cho-co-late!
Marcel I don't want it.
Charlotte Fine!
Marcel What time is it?
Charlotte It's half-past twelve!
Marcel So what?
Charlotte You said that already. What time would you like lunch, monsieur?
Marcel Eight o'clock.
Charlotte Very good, monsieur. When Monsieur engaged me, yesterday morning, he gave me specific instructions to wake him at nine o'clock.
Marcel Then there's still another eight and a half hours to go!
Charlotte I didn't realize you meant nine o'clock at night.
Marcel Fool!
Charlotte Yes, monsieur.

She exits

There is a long pause during which Marcel tries to go back to sleep. He tosses and turns

Marcel I'll fire her. That'll teach her not to wake me up! Can't she see I'm asleep. (*Beat*) Oh well! I suppose I should get up. (*He gets out of bed*) My socks! What did I do with my socks? Ah, here they are. (*He puts on his socks and slippers without sitting down, leaning against the foot of the bed*) Half-past twelve! I had a meeting at eleven! Still it was only a creditor, he's been waiting for six months so another hour won't do him any harm. Besides

I've nothing to give him! He'll find out soon enough! (*Still talking he opens the curtains*) It's already light! At half-past twelve! (*He turns out the night-light*) Where's my maid? What's she waiting for? Where's my chocolate? (*He rings the electric bell and keeping his finger on it begins to fall asleep again. He loses his balance and wakes up*) Only a sadist would ring like that! (*Realizing*) Oh, it's me. Damn it's cold. (*Taking off his slippers*) I'll have breakfast in bed and get up later. (*He slips back into bed with his socks but as he stretches out his feet meet an obstacle*) What on earth . . . What can this be? (*He stretches further*) What's this in my bed? We'll have to find out.

On his knees he draws back the covers and cries out when he sees Amélie who has slipped down to the foot of the bed and is still asleep. He seizes her by her wrist and pulls her up into a sitting position

Ah! Amélie! It's Amélie.

Amélie (*half-asleep*) Brrr! It's cold!

Marcel Amélie! It's Amélie!

Amélie (*yawning*) Hoooaah!

Marcel What are you doing here?

Amélie What? Oh God! (*She tries to go back to sleep*)

Marcel You can't go back to sleep. Amélie! Amélie!

He hears Charlotte returning, lets go of Amélie's wrist. She flops back on to the bed and he covers her with his pillow which he lounges on adopting a nonchalant air

Don't move!

Charlotte enters

Charlotte Did Monsieur ring?

Marcel Yes. Get out!

Charlotte Is that what you rang to tell me?

Marcel Yes!

Charlotte This is a wonderful job!

She exits

Marcel (*jumping to his knees and raising Amélie*) Quick, quick, Amélie. For goodness' sake!

Amélie (*yawning*) Hoooaah!

Marcel Wake up! For heaven's sake!

Amélie What's the matter?

Marcel Amélie, please! For God's sake.

Amélie (*opening her eyes*) What? Good God! Marcel!

Marcel Yes, Marcel! It's me Marcel!

Amélie What are you doing here?

Marcel You're asking me?!

Amélie I don't understand.

Marcel What are you doing here, in my house? In my bed? In my night-shirt?

Amélie In your bed? So I am! How did that happen?

Marcel That's what I'd like to know!

Amélie Did we . . .?
Marcel What?
Amélie Do you think we . . .?
Marcel It certainly looks like it.
Amélie Yes it does.
Marcel But that's appalling! You've been entrusted to my care.
Amélie Ah!
Marcel What shall I tell Étienne?
Amélie You don't have to tell him anything.
Marcel But the burden will be too great for my conscience. If I confess
  everything . . .
Amélie You'll hurt him terribly!
Marcel Yes, but it'll be a weight off my mind! How on earth did we come to
  do this?
Amélie I don't know. I can't remember a thing.
Marcel Étienne! My best friend! "Keep an eye on Amélie", he said. "I know
  I can be sure of her!"
Amélie Oh, trying to muzzle me eh! That just goes to prove what kind of trust
  he has in me.
Marcel Well, he's right isn't he!
Amélie He couldn't have thought this was going to happen. He had no right
  to suspect me, so it serves him right.
Marcel If he wasn't my best friend it would be so easy. I'm just a man who
  spent a night with a young lady . . . It happens every day!
Amélie Night actually.
Marcel True!
Amélie Anyway, if he hadn't been your best friend he wouldn't have put me
  in your hands.
Marcel (*changing tone*) So it's all his own fault!
Amélie Fancy telling you to "look after me". I'm going to get my own back!
Marcel What does he take me for? A eunuch! Doesn't he think I'm built the
  same way as him? Doesn't he go to bed with you?
Amélie All the time.
Marcel Well then . . .
Amélie Yes?
Marcel (*with contempt for his friend*) Pui!
Amélie Pui!

A pause during which they look at each other

Marcel All the same it's not on.
Amélie No.
Marcel He did have absolute faith in me and he did say . . .
Amélie "Keep an eye on Amélie".
Marcel We didn't even know we were doing it.
Amélie These things happen!
Marcel What were we doing yesterday evening?
Amélie We dined at Maxime's, then we dined again au Pied de Cochon and
  then we went to drink champagne at Pigalle . . .

Marcel And then we went to the Royal for iced kümmel.
Amélie And then, and then fireworks—puiii . . . it all gets a little more hazy.
  I can make out more bars and lots of lights . . . more champagne!
Marcel And then . . .
Amélie And then nothing. Black obscurity.
Marcel (*turning the bottle upside down*) Nothing! But what happened . . .?
  Did we or didn't we? What's important is that Étienne should remain as
  ignorant as us.
Amélie And *we're* not going to tell him.
Marcel So, nothing happened.
Amélie Nothing.
Marcel Nothing!
Amélie Lucky Étienne.
Marcel We've worried ourselves silly over something that never happened!
Amélie (*throwing herself on to the bed*) I feel so lazy!
Marcel Come on. Up, up, up!
Amélie Oh you're so boring. (*She screams*) Ah!
Marcel What is it?
Amélie I went to bed in my boots!
Marcel Very funny.
Amélie I'm not laughing, my dear. I'm shocked.
Marcel Where is your dress?
Amélie I don't know.
Marcel (*finding her hat*) Here's your hat. And your mask next to it.
Amélie Really?

He puts the mask on making Amélie laugh

Marcel Ah, your dress.
Amélie On the table!
Marcel (*still masked with her hat under his left arm*) Is that a nice place to
  hang a dress?
Amélie My hat!
Marcel I beg your pardon! (*He takes the hat from under his armpit and puts it
  on his head*)
Amélie Marcel, give me my hat!
Marcel (*putting the hat on her head*) You've got your priorities right. (*He
  takes her dress from the table*) Go on, quickly! Mush, mush! (*As he goes he
  gets his feet caught in the dress—angrily*) Get a move on! Mush! Mush!

He exits

Amélie Mush, mush! I've no intention of mushing! (*She puts her legs to the
  floor*) Oh, my legs feel like jelly! Courage, Amélie! Where's my petticoat?

Charlotte enters

  Oh!
Charlotte I beg your pardon!
Amélie Oh! I was just . . .
Charlotte Are you waiting for Monsieur Courbois?

Amélie What? Yes, yes exactly.

Charlotte I don't know if Monsieur is accepting visitors; I'll go and find out.

Amélie (*parading in front of Charlotte as though a night-shirt was the latest Parisian fashion*) Don't trouble yourself. I'll call again, mademoiselle!

Marcel enters hurriedly

Marcel There, now if you——(*To Charlotte*) What are you doing here?

Charlotte Madame here wanted——

Marcel Madame?

Charlotte She wanted to know if Monsieur was at home.

Amélie rubs up against him cheekily

Marcel Who gave you permission to come in?

Charlotte (*presenting him with a packet of papers and letters*) The concierge has just brought the post up.

Marcel Is that any reason to wander in here as though it were a café? Give me those and get out.

Charlotte (*giving him the packet and a large ball of string*) Here! The writing paper and the ball of string you asked me to buy yesterday, monsieur.

Marcel Put it on the night table! Can't you see my hands are full?

Charlotte Yes, monsieur.

Marcel And bring a bottle of champagne!

Charlotte Yes monsieur.

Marcel Pui!

Charlotte Yes monsieur.

Charlotte exits

Marcel Pui!

Amélie I think she spotted me! (*She laughs*)

Marcel She's bright! I'll have to get rid of her.

Amélie What's she called?

Marcel I don't know.

Amélie You don't know your own maid's name?

Marcel She arrived yesterday morning when I was still asleep. I employed her in the dark. This is the first time I've seen her.

Amélie If I were your mistress I don't think I'd let you have a maid like that. She's too pretty for a bachelor.

Marcel Don't be silly. Go and get dressed. (*Dragging her to the door*) Your things are in there.

Amélie All right! Just a minute . . .

Marcel What now?

Amélie I can't put on my dress.

Marcel Why not?

Amélie It's a low-cut evening gown. I can't go out in the daylight in that.

Marcel You can travel by Metro.

Amélie No, no! I'd look silly. I'll write a note to Papa and ask him to bring me a proper dress; you can have your maid deliver the letter! Now she's seen me, there's nothing to hide.

Marcel (*resignedly*) All right. But we're wasting time!

Amélie (*as she writes*) "Little father, I am at Marcel Courbois' in the Rue Cambon, where I have been staying overnight. Come and fetch me and bring me a dress. Hugs and kisses. Amélie." Now for the address: Monsieur Pochet.

Marcel (*who has opened one of his letters*) Ah!

Amélie Rue de Rivoli. What's the matter?

Marcel Oh God.

Amélie What is it?

Marcel My godfather! My godfather's coming back to Paris!

Amélie Van Putzeboum?

Marcel Why's he coming? He left for good.

Amélie A flying visit?

Marcel Listen to his letter. "Little godsonny"—you remember he's from Rotenburg. "Little godsonny"—he lives in Holland——

Amélie But he's from Rotenburg.

Marcel Did I tell you?

Amélie Yes! Go on.

Marcel "Little godsonny. Am I a surprise for you. I am in Paris since this morning. This afternoon am I seeing you. I do love surprises."

Amélie So do I!

Marcel "PS. We ought to dine tonight with your fiancée and her father, Monsieur d'Avranches."

Amélie I can't tonight.

Marcel But we ought! We ought!

Amélie But tonight I'm dining with——

Marcel Cancel it! Ought means will!

Amélie Fine! I'll put off my dining companion, but I don't think it's funny.

Marcel We ought, dear Amélie. We ought!

Amélie (*as she begins writing on a second sheet*) All right! All right!

Marcel I thought I was well rid of him. He's supposed to have left for America.

Amélie Well perhaps that's it!

Marcel What?

Amélie If he's leaving for America . . .

Marcel Yes?

Amélie He's got to embark at Le Havre . . .

Marcel So?

Amélie It's only natural he should come via Paris. (*She has taken an envelope and writes the address*)

Marcel And he'll probably be gone tomorrow.

Amélie Probably.

Marcel Thank God. (*He rings the bell*)

Amélie Wait. It's not dry.

Marcel Blow on it. (*She blows on both envelopes and puts a letter in each*) Come in!

Charlotte puts her head round the door

Charlotte Is it all right to come in?

Marcel What?
Charlotte I know Monsieur rang but does he really want me to come in?
Marcel Are you pulling my leg?
Charlotte No, monsieur.
Marcel Fool!
Charlotte Yes monsieur.
Marcel Madame has an errand for you.
Amélie This letter is to go to the Continental Hotel——
Charlotte Yes madame.
Amélie Wait a minute! And this one to the rue de Rivoli.
Charlotte So it's not an errand!
Marcel What do you mean it's not an errand?
Charlotte It's two errands!
Marcel Get out of my sight!
Charlotte Yes monsieur.
Marcel Out!
Charlotte (*running*) Yes monsieur!
Marcel Fool.

Charlotte exits

Amélie (*to herself as she returns to bed*) Oh, I'm freezing!
Marcel (*of Charlotte*) You're a fool. (*Seeing Amélie in bed*) What! No, no. You can't go back to bed.
Amélie But I'm frozen. Just while I wait for Papa . . .
Marcel Just while I wait for Papa indeed! Come on, get up! Up!
Amélie Oh please, Marcel!
Marcel Up, up, up!

There is a ring at the doorbell

Damn. There's someone at the door.
Amélie Yes.
Marcel Who's coming to disturb us now?
Charlotte (*off*) Who did you say you wanted, madame?
Irene (*off*) Isn't Monsieur at home?
Marcel Oh God! It's Irene!
Amélie Who?
Marcel My mistress! Quick, move!
Amélie Do you mean Madame?
Marcel (*pulling her out of bed*) Good God, don't you understand. Get out of here! Hide!
Amélie Where? Where?
Marcel (*undoing the curtain ropes*) I don't know. Under the bed! Hurry, for God's sake!
Amélie (*sliding under the bed*) I'm beginning to remember what happened last night!
Marcel Will you hurry? For goodness sake! (*He draws the curtains and jumps on to the bed as there is a knock at the door*)

Irene enters

Irene May I come in?
Marcel (*as if just waking up*) Who is it?
Irene It's so dark in here.
Marcel Who's there?
Irene Doesn't your heart tell you?
Marcel (*trying to speak tenderly but quavering*) Oh Irene!
Irene (*as she gropes her way towards the bed*) His heart told him. Ah chéri . . .
where are you?
Marcel Here!

Irene puts her hand on his face

Oh!
Irene Oh did I stick my finger in your eye?
Marcel In my mouth actually!
Irene My darling!
Marcel My little Rene!

They kiss

Amélie (*her face appearing from below the bed*) It's not much fun under here!

Irene gropes for the light switch

Irene It's so gloomy in here! I can't see a thing! And you can't see me. (*She
knocks the ball of string off the table*) Oh what have I dropped? It's gone
under the bed. Just a minute!
Amélie Whoops!
Marcel Leave it!
Irene But it's gone under the bed!
Marcel It's only a ball of string. I'll get it later.
Irene Just as you like.
Amélie What a shame! I nearly had company.
Irene (*finding the switch*) There! At last! Now we can see each other!
Marcel It's high time I got up. (*He puts his legs out of bed*)
Irene (*putting his legs back on to the bed*) Why do you say that?
Marcel (*putting his legs out*) Well it's high time isn't it?
Irene (*putting his legs in*) Not at all. I've just arrived and you want to get up!
Here I am, next to you, beside myself with happiness, quivering with desire
for you . . .
Marcel (*with a feeble smile*) Aha?
Irene Like husband and wife!
Marcel Aha?
Irene Happy?
Marcel Yes! Oh yes, yes!
Amélie Here we go!
Irene And we can do everything a husband and wife do!
Marcel Aha?
Amélie Not bouncy-bouncy. Please!

Irene My darling. My darling!
Marcel Rene, my Rene!
Amélie Curtain up!
Marcel (*aside*) Three's a crowd.
Irene I can spend the rest of the day with you!
Amélie What?
Marcel (*terrified*) Aha?
Amélie That means me too.
Marcel The whole day?
Irene You don't seem overjoyed.
Marcel Me? Oh yes, yes. Yes!
Irene Here I am next to you . . .
Marcel Yes! I knew there was something. I have to take a bath. Come on, come to the bathroom with me . . . (*He tries to get out of bed*)
Irene What are you talking about?
Marcel You don't want to come to the bathroom?
Irene Of course I don't.
Amélie He'll have to do better than that.
Irene Why on earth should we go to the bathroom? You are going to go beddy-byes and I'm going to take all my clothes off and go beddy-byes too. (*She goes to the table to undo her collar*)
Marcel (*anxiously*) Aha?
Amélie So much for countesses.
Irene (*grappling with the hooks on the back of her dress*) Oh these hooks! Help me please, Marcel!

He doesn't respond

Marcel! Whatever is the matter?
Marcel Pardon?
Irene Is something wrong?
Marcel No! No!
Irene You're in another world! Would it by any chance be something to do with your visits to Mademoiselle d'Avranches?
Amélie Me!
Marcel Who? What? What do you mean?
Irene I knew this business of borrowing a fiancée to satisfy your godfather would end like this.
Marcel Me and Amélie! Surely you don't believe such a thing?
Amélie (*lying in view flat on her back she hits the mattress little blows with her fists*) Go on! Tell her, tell her!
Irene I hope not. Anyway she's not your sort. So saucy.
Marcel (*hitting the mattress in turn*) Saucy, yes saucy.
Amélie (*seizing his wrist and causing him to almost fall out of bed*) You're too kind.
Marcel (*trying to regain his balance*) Ah!
Irene (*catching hold of his leg*) What on earth is the matter with you?
Marcel The mattress is slipping.
Irene (*shrugging*) Oh! (*She turns her back on him*)

Marcel, profiting from her lack of attention hits Amélie on the back while she, on all fours, is trying to scramble back under the bed

Amélie Oh!

Irene What?

Marcel Nothing. Nothing! I just went "oh".

Irene After all what's so special about Amélie? She's an ex-chambermaid. A cleaner!

Amélie Here we go!

Irene Common . . . uncultured!

Amélie Go on. I can take it!

Irene I mean her hands, have you seen her hands?

Marcel No, no I——

Amélie (*looking at her hands*) What's wrong with my hands?

Irene She's a good girl but very unkempt . . .

Amélie She's beginning to annoy me.

Irene She waves her hair with vanilla essence, my dear. Didn't you notice?

Amélie I'm not going to stay down here listening to this. (*She disappears underneath the bed*)

Irene No, the only real woman for you is me.

Amélie Right! That does it!

As Irene lights the night-light

Marcel What are you doing?

Irene There are times when I prefer the dark. (*She turns out the light*)

Amélie The ball of string! Of course!

She disappears below the bed again and during the following one sees her hands manipulating the coverlet which hangs over the foot of the bed, as she ties string to it. Then she exits to the dressing-room

Irene (*jumping into bed*) Oh darling, my darling!

Marcel Oh Rene, my little Rene.

They kiss

Irene Oh I like it in your bed. If you only knew what a bad night I've had.

Marcel Not as bad as mine! I worked late into the night.

Irene I had nightmares. I was drowsing. Suddenly I woke and saw a floating white figure waving its arms . . . Oh I do adore you.

Marcel Yes, yes, but what was it?

Irene My husband in his night-shirt. I was haunted by it all night! The eiderdown's fallen off!

Marcel It doesn't matter.

Irene And all night long I seemed to see objects moving about, the furniture walking.

She screams as she sees the eiderdown apparently move of its own accord across the room in a series of jerks

Ah!

She jumps over Marcel to the far side of the room while the eiderdown continues to jerk its way towards the dressing-room

Aaaaaaaaah!

Marcel What is it?

Irene There! There! Your eiderdown's moving!

Marcel (*aside*) That bitch Amélie. (*Innocently*) Where? I can't see anything.

Irene It's my nightmare all over again. Oh, Marcel, I'm frightened.

Marcel Calm down! Just because an eiderdown goes for a walk. It happens every day. Only yesterday I saw one on the Champs-Elysées.

Irene Did you Marcel? Aaaaaaah!

Marcel What is it?

Irene There! It's coming back!

Marcel What!

Irene There! There!

Marcel It's coming back on its own.

Irene Aaaaaaah!

Marcel Don't panic! Stay calm! Let's be calm about this! (*He approaches the eiderdown*)

Irene No, Marcel, don't go near it!

Marcel (*hesitating momentarily at her scream*) Let's not panic! (*He tiptoes towards the eiderdown*) Come on, Marcel. Courage!

Irene Marcel, take care. I beg you!

Marcel A man's got to do what a man's got to do. (*He approaches the eiderdown with great circumspection and kicks at it with his feet. Eventually seizing his courage in both hands he takes hold of it by one corner and shakes it. He takes it over to Irene in triumph*) There! You see. No need to be frightened.

Irene You're so brave!

Marcel A man should never run away, not even from an eiderdown!

At this moment the eiderdown jumps from his grasp and in one jerk lands back on the foot of the bed

Irene ⎫
Marcel ⎬ (*together*) Aaaaaaah!

Irene Oh my God! Help! Help!

Marcel Stop screaming! You'll make me lose my nerve!

Irene It's bewitched!

Marcel Stop screaming! Stop screaming.

Irene rushes towards the dressing-room just as . . .

Amélie enters, wearing the mask and dressed in a bathing robe, the cowl pulled over her head looking like a monstrous gnome. She holds a lighted sparkler in each hand and advances into the room with little lop-sided steps

Irene Help! Heeelp!

Charlotte enters

Charlotte What is it? What's the matter? (*Seeing the gnome*) Aaaaah! Help! Help!

Both Irene and Charlotte exit

Marcel (*as panic-stricken as the women*) Quict! Be quiet! (*Alone, terrified*) Spare me! Have pity!

Amélie takes off her costume and throws it into the dressing-room

Amélie Well, I think that served its purpose!

Marcel It's you!

Amélie Why Marcel, what are you doing on the floor?

Marcel Do you know what agony you've caused those women?

Amélie If it weren't for me she'd still be here and you'd be tying yourself up in knots trying to explain. That'll teach her to insult me! My hands indeed! What's wrong with my hands? (*She goes to the bed to extinguish the night-light and climbs into bed*)

Marcel No, no, you can't go back to sleep. Get up, come on. Up, up, up!

Amélie Not even now?

Marcel Up!

There is a ring at the doorbell

Amélie Somebody's at the door.

Marcel Yes.

Van Putzeboum (*off*) Admission please! Unblock! I'm his godfather.

Marcel My God. It's him! Go on, get out! Out!

Amélie Where?

Marcel Under the bed, quick!

Amélie Not again!

Marcel Quick.

The door handle is turned

Too late!

Marcel jumps on to the bed and covers both himself and Amélie with the bedclothes as . . .

Van Putzeboum enters

Van Putzeboum (*who has caught sight of the movement under the bedclothes; aside*) Just a moment! (*He tiptoes to the bed and throws back the bedclothes*)

Marcel 〕 (*together*) There's no room!
Amélie 〕

Van Putzeboum (*dumbfounded*) Goodbye, Mademoiselle d'Avranches!

Amélie I just happened to be in the area!

Marcel (*to Amélie*) Oh it's you! (*Offering his hand*) How are you?

Amélie (*shaking his hand*) What a lovely surprise!

Van Putzeboum In bed together!

Marcel You could look it at like that!

Amélie I was just passing by!

Van Putzeboum Bye-byes. Yes. I see. I see.
Marcel What do you mean?
Van Putzeboum All right, little godsonny?
Marcel Not bad, Godfather.
Van Putzeboum Was it good, eh? Eh?
Marcel Godfather!
Van Putzeboum Gotferdeck! Leaping the gun.
Amélie ⎫
Marcel ⎰ (*together*) What?
Van Putzeboum Eh, little godsonny?
Marcel Godfather, you must let me explain——
Amélie Monsieur, I assure you——
Van Putzeboum Oh it's no matter! It's your business anyway!
Marcel Yes of course, but——
Van Putzeboum Taste the wine first. That's up to you. (*Going towards the bed*) And how is the young financée?
Amélie You can see how I am, Godfather.
Van Putzeboum My, my, my. Only a fortnight ago, like the lamb from Mary.
Amélie Me!
Van Putzeboum As they say here in Paris "Faint heart never catched the early bird".
Amélie Oh!
Van Putzeboum (*playfully punching Marcel in the stomach knocking him on to the sofa*) The young devil. And what about her farter, Monsieur d'Avranches? What's he got to say about all this then?
Marcel Oh, he doesn't know a thing! We wouldn't tell him . . . we wouldn't tell anybody in fact. Nobody. Not a soul!
Van Putzeboum Don't worry now. What do you think I am, eh? I am not splitting.
Amélie Besides there's nothing to tell. We were only sleeping.
Van Putzeboum Yes, yes and I aroused you. I must beg your pardon, but I didn't know, did I?
Amélie But——
Van Putzeboum I wanted my return to be a surprise.
Marcel It was certainly that.
Van Putzeboum I said to myself "In memory of his farter and for the love I owe him, I can't let the little godsonny get married without me."
Marcel Pardon?
Van Putzeboum I've sent representatives to take my place in America and I'll join him there after the wedding. Are you delightful?
Marcel Wed . . . Wed . . . Wed . . .
Van Putzeboum Wed . . . Wed . . . Wed . . . have you a speech impediment?
Marcel No. I was repeating "after the wedding"?
Van Putzeboum Yes. I'll be able to give you your inheritance in my person.
Marcel (*collapsing on the sofa*) What a surprise.
Van Putzeboum Aren't you delightful?
Marcel Yes delightful.

Van Putzeboum I hoped you would be. Well this won't buy the baby a new bathtub. (*He goes over to the bed*) Now that I've seen you I think your financée could get dressed, don't you? And I'm in the way.

Marcel (*fetching Van Putzeboum's hat and cane and pressing them on him*) You're going already? Well never mind!

Van Putzeboum Yes, I've got a lot of to do. I'll fetch both of you in half an hour. Then we can take a promenade before dinner, eh?

Marcel (*pushing him towards the door*) Absolutely.

Amélie You're spoiling us.

Van Putzeboum It's my pleasure my dear. I know the best cookers in Paris—you will let Papa know that he's dining with us.

Marcel Of course.

Van Putzeboum I've gone. Don't trouble yourself, Please. Hallo!

Marcel Hallo! Hallo!

Van Putzeboum exits

It's a catastrophe!

Amélie Come on, it's not all over yet.

Marcel What do you mean? The one thing I can't provide is a real wedding.

Amélie Not easy.

Van Putzeboum enters

Van Putzeboum Farter's here. It's your farter.

Marcel What?

Amélie Whose farter?

Van Putzeboum Yours. He's coming up the stairs.

Marcel So?

Van Putzeboum Aren't you going to hide? Quick now!

Amélie Me!

Van Putzeboum If he sees you like that, he'll suspect something. Go and hide!

Marcel Yes, yes.

Van Putzeboum (*pushing Amélie towards the dressing-room*) Go in there!

Amélie My favourite prison!

She exits as . . .

Pochet bursts in

Pochet Ah, there you are.

Marcel You!

Pochet Is my daughter here?

Marcel Amélie?

Van Putzeboum No, Monsieur. She isn't here.

Pochet She isn't here?

Van Putzeboum No, I've been in every crook and nanny of the apartment; she isn't here.

Marcel Don't be ridiculous, she's——

Van Putzeboum He doesn't know quite what he's saying. But he's a gentleman is Marcel, and he doesn't forget that a ladle is a ladle.

Pochet "A ladle is a ladle"? What do you mean? (*To Marcel*) Well, no matter. I must talk to you.

Marcel (*trying to drag Van Putzeboum towards the door*) Godfather? My dear godfather . . .

Van Putzeboum What is it?

Marcel Weren't you going to go for a walk?

Van Putzeboum (*to Marcel*) Careful, Marcel. Her farter smells a mouse. If I leave you now . . .

Marcel Don't worry.

Van Putzeboum I try to get her out without her farter seeing.

Marcel No, no. Leave it to me.

Van Putzeboum It's up to you then. I'm only thinking of your future.

Marcel I'm deeply grateful.

Van Putzeboum At least try to lay a little.

Marcel Yes, yes. Don't worry.

Van Putzeboum Hallo then. Until later! Monsieur d'Avranches, we're dining together this evening, are we not?

Pochet Me?

Van Putzeboum Yes, I arranged it with Marcel and your daughter.

Pochet So you have seen her then?

Van Putzeboum What? No. But I just presumed that as my godsonny was dining with me so would his financée.

Pochet I see.

Van Putzeboum (*to Marcel*) I'm going. It's safer if I leave.

Marcel It certainly is. Hallo.

Van Putzeboum Hallo!

Van Putzeboum exits

Pochet What does all this mean? He's come back, has he?

Marcel Like a bad smell.

Pochet For long?

Marcel Until the wedding. He wants to attend.

Pochet That's bad luck. What are you going to do?

Marcel How should I know?

Pochet What a shame! It was such a good idea. But if it goes on much longer it'll compromise Amélie.

Marcel How so?

Pochet If people really believe that she's engaged it'll put them off her.

Marcel Oh!

Pochet She didn't come home last night.

Marcel (*playing along*) Really?

Pochet I swear it! I don't like it at all.

Amélie enters

Amélie Good-morning, Papa.

Pochet You are here, after all!

Amélie You knew I was.

Pochet He said you weren't. (*To Marcel*) What do you mean?

Marcel It wasn't me. It was my godfather!

Amélie You knew where I was anyway. I wrote to you.

Pochet To me?

Amélie Yes. Haven't you brought me a suit of clothes?

Pochet Was I supposed to?

Amélie Yes, to wear now. All I've got is an evening gown.

Pochet (*looking at the night-shirt*) So . . . I see. But I didn't receive anything. Your note must have arrived after I'd left.

Amélie So why did you come here?

Pochet To warn you! In case he were to drop round.

Amélie } (*together*) Who?
Marcel }

Pochet Étienne!

Amélie } (*together*) Étienne?
Marcel }

Pochet He's completed his military service.

Marcel In a fortnight?

Pochet Mumps!

Marcel Mumps?

Pochet His regiment caught it! An epidemic!

Marcel Oh my God!

Pochet He turned up at the house just now.

Marcel Oh my God!

Amélie What did you tell him?

Pochet I told him that you'd gone out early.

Amélie Very likely.

Pochet What else could I say? A nice thing—making your father lie. I used to take solemn oaths in the Witness Box.

Amélie It's only once.

Pochet I don't like it at all. And as for spending the night away from home!

Amélie Oh Papa! Don't blame me. I did spend the night here, but——

Pochet I don't wish to know. (*To Marcel*) I don't wish to know.

Marcel I'm not going to tell you!

Pochet I never meddle in your affairs. There are certain things in life where a self-respecting father must keep his distance. I have never wanted to sit in judgement on you. Isn't that true?

Amélie True.

Pochet But I will say this: never in my life, apart from the days when I was on nights, never have I spent the night away from home. (*To Marcel*) Never!

Marcel I didn't say anything.

Pochet (*softening*) If I had moments of weakness they were generally in the afternoons.

Amélie Much more convenient.

Pochet Quite!

Amélie But Papa, it wasn't entirely our fault. Yesterday evening we must have drunk six bottles of champagne!

Marcel It's surprising we're not hung over!

Amélie It's a miracle.

Pochet (*putting his arm round both Amélie's and Marcel's shoulders, he kisses Amélie and turns instinctively to do the same to Marcel but stops*) Ah well! Youthful folly!

There is a noise off

Prince (*off*) Landlord!
Marcel Who's that in the hall? (*He opens the door to peek out and closes it immediately*) Good God! It's the Prince! In my house!
Pochet The Prince! Here!
Amélie And I'm in your night-shirt! (*She runs to the curtain and drapes herself in it*)
Pochet Oh, my God! Where's the candelabra? (*He seizes the candlestick which is on the bureau*)

The Prince enters

Prince So many people.
Pochet Sire!
Prince Ah, the father! Still got your candle!
Pochet Yes, sire.
Prince But why are you always holding a candle? Are you a compulsive candle-holder?
Pochet No sire. It's for you.
Prince And please. I'm not "sire"! Plain "sir" will do. Did you receive your decoration?
Pochet Yes, from your most majestic Highness himself, sire.
Prince Good. (*He turns his back on him*)

Pochet puts the candlestick on the table

Marcel (*aside*) What's he doing here?
Prince Where is Mademoiselle d'Avranches?
Pochet Amélie, Amélie! His Highness is calling you! Come on out dearest.
Amélie No!
Pochet When a king commands! (*To the Prince*) She's hiding, the dear child!
Prince Hiding! Please, Mademoiselle d'Avranches!
Amélie Oh sir!
Pochet (*to the Prince*) She's not dressed.
Amélie (*being presented by her Father and still draped in the curtain*) Sir, I'm still in my night-dress.
Prince You were expecting me then?
Amélie Was I?
Pochet (*in the Prince's ear*) She's a poppet. It's not surprising that a crowned head——
Prince Here! (*Handing him his hat*) Take it and be quiet!
Pochet Forgive me.
Prince You wrote asking me to come and here I am.
Amélie I did?
Prince The general's following me, with dresses!
Amélie What!

Prince I told him to bring a selection . . . as I didn't know your measurements.
Amélie But sir, there must be a mistake. I didn't put that in your letter.
Prince Here it is. (*He takes the letter out of his pocket and reads*) "Little father"—I like that—"I am at Marcel Courbois' in the Rue Cambon."
Amélie (*indicating Marcel*) This is him!
Prince Monsieur.
Marcel (*who has absent-mindedly taken up the candle. He bows deeply*) Sir!
Prince That candle again!
Amélie This is Monsieur Courbois.
Prince The landlord!
Marcel What?
Prince Very good.
Marcel (*to Pochet*) What does he mean, the landlord?
Pochet Quiet.
Prince (*to Amélie*) Where was I? Oh yes. "Come and fetch me and bring me a dress."
Amélie But sir. I didn't write that letter to you.
Prince What?
Amélie I was writing to Papa.
Prince I don't understand.
Amélie I must have put the wrong letter in the envelope!
Pochet So I received the letter intended for your Highness.
Prince (*making a noise to impose silence*) Ah! . . . Ah! . . . Ah! . . . Mademoiselle can explain things herself.
Amélie But sir, I wouldn't have called you "little father".
Marcel She wouldn't have been so familiar.
Prince Ah! . . . Ah! . . . Ah!
Marcel Sorry!
Prince Why are you interfering, landlord?
Marcel (*aside*) Landlord!
Pochet Just so. One does not speak to a Royal Prince before he speaks to you. (*To the Prince*) Aren't I right, sir?
Prince You should know.
Pochet That's what I told him.
Prince Practise what you preach!
Pochet Oh! Right!
Prince (*to Amélie*) On the contrary. I thought it was charming to be called little father. It's tender and affectionate! It's Slavonic. I enjoy familiarity because I have a horror of etiquette and protocol.
Pochet (*to Amélie*) There, you see!
Prince Ah! . . . Ah! . . . Ah! . . .
Pochet Sorry!
Prince I like to laugh, to be amused, to play tricks.
Pochet I sympathize.
Prince Ah! . . . Ah! (*To Amélie*) Tell me, do you know the great Patchikoff?
Amélie No.
Pochet No, we——

Prince I was asking Mademoiselle.
Pochet Yes, but I know she doesn't know him.
Prince Ah! . . . Ah! . . . Ah! . . .
Marcel One does not speak to a Royal Prince before he speaks to you.
Pochet (*like the Prince*) Ah! . . . Ah! . . . Ah!
Prince Patchikoff was a chamberlain at my court. Well the other evening after dinner four of my officers tied him up, took him by the arms and legs and threw him into a bath full of icy water.
Amélie Really?
Prince He was furious. He didn't dare say anything, but he was furious. Oh we laughed! Did we laugh! And now he's dead . . . congestion of the lungs.

Amélie ⎫
     (*together*) No!
Pochet ⎭

Pochet How funny!
Marcel (*aside*) This Prince is a fool!
Pochet Very funny, very funny indeed!
Prince Listen, little father, I've given you a decoration. Now you leave us in peace!

There is a ring at the doorbell

 The bell! It must be the general! Go and see, landlord!
Marcel (*aside*) What does he take me for? A flunkey?

The door opens and Charlotte shows in the General followed by a Shop Assistant carrying a box. The General, finding Marcel next to the door hands him his hat

Marcel (*aside*) Charming!
Prince General, come in!
Koshnadieff Your Highness!
Prince Did you bring the dresses?
Koshnadieff These are all I could find, sir. (*To the Assistant*) Put them there, man. (*To the Prince*) I got them on sale or return. (*To the Assistant*) That's it. Dismissed. You can take the rest back later.

The Assistant exits

Prince (*to Amélie*) Now my dear, would you like to look?
Amélie Sir! (*She makes courtly gestures to the Prince and catching her heel in the box almost falls*) Sir!
Prince (*reading the label on the box*) Trois Quartiers. Will that do?
Amélie Trois Quartiers! My God. I mean sir.
Prince Perhaps you'd like to try some on?
Amélie If somebody would be so kind as to bring them through there. (*Indicating the dressing-room*)

Pochet is about to pick up the box

Prince Ah! . . . Ah! . . . Ah!
Amélie Oh Prince, not the General!
Prince That's what he's there for!

The General is flattered: he salutes proudly

Amélie I'm overwhelmed.
Koshnadieff Please, mademoiselle.
Amélie This way then, General.

Amélie exits

The General tries to fit the box through the doorway lengthways

Pochet Not that way, General. This way.
Koshnadieff Kolaschnik!

Koshnadieff exits

Marcel What did he say?
Pochet Kolaschnik!

He exits after him

Prince What do you want?
Marcel If your Highness will allow me, I'd like to get dressed too.
Prince Why should that interest me?
Marcel You asked me what I wanted.
Prince This is your place, is it?
Marcel It certainly is.
Prince Ugly.
Marcel Pardon.
Prince Ugly.
Marcel (*aside*) Is he having me on?
Prince Very ugly.
Marcel I wouldn't say that! Considering the rent.
Prince Which is?
Marcel (*not understanding*) Sir?
Prince Which is?
Marcel (*still not understanding*) Which is?
Prince What do you rent it at?
Marcel Oh! Eighteen hundred francs.
Prince A day?
Marcel A day! No, a year.
Prince Good heavens!
Marcel Not bad for eighteen hundred francs, eh?
Prince And what does that make each day?
Marcel What?
Prince Each day?
Marcel What's each day's rent, you mean?
Prince Yes.
Marcel I see. (*Aside*) What an odd question.
Prince Well?
Marcel A hundred and fifty francs a month is a hundred sous per day.
Simple! That's five francs! Five francs a day!
Prince You rent it at five francs a day?

Marcel Yes.

Prince For five francs a day you can't expect the Doge's Palace!

Marcel I wouldn't know what to do with it.

Prince Five francs a day is fine. Tell the General.

Marcel The General? What should I tell him?

Prince That it's five francs a day!

Marcel Why should he care?

Prince It's his job.

Marcel (*aside*) Hasn't he got anything better to do with his time?

Pochet enters

Pochet She's made her choice.

Prince Very good!

Koshnadieff enters

Koshnadieff!

Koshnadieff Highness?

Prince Moia moarowna! Tetaieff polna coramal momalsk scrowno? (Come here a minute. Did she find a dress she wanted?)

Koshnadieff Stchi! A spanie co tenia, sir, co rassa ta swa lop! (One that fits like a glove, sir.)

Prince Very good!

Koshnadieff Swoya Aletessia na bouk papelskoyya mimi? (Has Your Highness any further need of me?)

Prince Nack. Woulia mawolsk twarla tschikkopna to the landlord, there?

Marcel "Landlord"!

Prince Quanti prencha. (Twenty francs.)

Koshnadieff Oh! Stchi!

Marcel (*to Pochet*) What was he saying about me?

Koshnadieff Quantchi prencha. Here you are!

Marcel What's this for?

Pochet Take it, take it. It's a louis.

Marcel A louis! (*To the Prince*) What do you want me to do with it?

Prince It's the rent.

Marcel The rent! Your Highness must be joking?

Prince What do you mean? You told me five francs and I've given you twenty.

Koshnadieff Twenty francs.

Marcel But I don't want this.

Prince What do you mean?

Marcel I don't keep a boarding house. Here, take it back!

Prince (*scandalized*) What?

Koshnadieff Don't upset his Highness.

Pochet Don't make a fuss.

Marcel I don't want his louis.

Pochet (*taking the louis from Marcel*) Well that's no reason for making so much fuss. (*To the Prince*) Forgive me sir . . . but this doesn't seem to know where it belongs. (*He puts the louis in his purse*)

Prince I am extremely displeased, do you understand? I shall never come back to this establishment again.

Pochet (*to Marcel*) There!

Marcel (*aside*) You said it!

Prince Now be off! I've had enough of you!

Marcel You want me to leave?

Pochet Yes, go on! We'll do better without you. (*To the Prince*) Won't we sir?

Prince Yes. And you too!

Pochet Me?

Prince Go on, both of you.

Pochet Very well.

Marcel (*laughing hysterically*) He's turning me out of my own house.

Pochet Come on now. (*Taking Marcel by the arm and leading him towards the dressing-room*) Let's do as he says.

Prince No!

Pochet ⎱ (*together*) What?
Marcel ⎰

Prince Not in there! I've rented that room.

Marcel (*laughing hysterically*) He's rented it! This is farcical!

Pochet Where shall we go?

Marcel I don't know. The laundry room!

Pochet The laundry room! We can count the sheets.

They exit

Marcel (*as he goes*) Yes, we'll just go and count the sheets.

Koshnadieff Swoya Aletessia na bouk papelskoya mimi? (Has your Highness any further need of me?)

Prince Nack. (No.)

Koshnadieff Lovo, sta Swoya Altessia lo madiet, me pipilska teradief. (If your Highness will allow, I should like to retire.)

Prince Bonadia Koshnadieff. (Good-day Koshnadieff.)

Koshnadieff Arwaloouck Motjarnie. (Goodbye, sir.)

Koshnadieff exits

Prince Why did she choose such an awful landlord?

There is a knock at the door

Come in.

Charlotte enters carrying a pair of folded sheets

The chambermaid! What do you want?

Charlotte I've come to make the bed.

Prince Come closer so that I can look at you properly. Pretty! In fact you're very pretty for a chambermaid.

Charlotte Thanks! But if you stay on the bed like that, I'll never be able to make it.

Prince I am Prince Nicolas of Palestrie.

Charlotte And I'm Charlotte. How do you do?

Prince (*taking the sheets from her arms and drawing her towards the bed, feeling her hips*) Come a little closer, so I can look at you properly.
Charlotte You are used to servants, then?
Prince (*sitting her on his knee*) Now my baby, what do you like?
Charlotte You're a funny old thing.
Prince (*bouncing her on his knee*) Now little baby, how's that?
Charlotte (*pinching his cheeks*) Oh big boy!
Prince Oh I like it when they show no respect. (*He pulls her on top of him*) Talk dirty to me Charlotte!

Amélie enters

Amélie Oh sire! I beg your pardon!
Prince (*sitting up*) Not at all, not at all! I was waiting for you. (*He gives Charlotte a slap on the bottom*) Go on, be off with you!
Charlotte That was a quick romance.

Charlotte exits

Prince Amélie.
Amélie I seem to have disturbed you, sir.
Prince Not a bit, not a bit! As you say in France: I was warming up before the match! Come here.
Amélie I am obedient in everything, sir!
Prince But why have you put on that dress?
Amélie Because it suits me.
Prince But why?
Amélie Because you told me sir.
Prince Ah well. We'll take it off bit by bit. (*He sits her on his knee*) Now my baby, what do you like?

Pochet enters

Pochet Quick, quick!

Marcel enters after him

Marcel Putzeboum! It's Putzeboum!
Prince What!
Amélie Putzeboum!
Prince What's Putzeboum? What is this Putzeboum? Are we never to be left in peace?
Amélie (*to Pochet*) Putzeboum! How do you know?
Pochet I saw him coming through the window.
Marcel He'll be here any second.
Amélie Oh my God!
Prince It makes no difference to us!
Amélie Oh yes it does, sir. He mustn't see you here.
Prince Why not? Is he a terrorist?
Amélie No!
Prince Then I couldn't care less.
Marcel Well we could!

There is a ring at the doorbell

Amélie ⎫
Pochet ⎬ *(together)*   The bell! It's him! Quick! Quick! Hurry, sir hurry. In
Marcel ⎭   there.
Amélie Sir, I beg you!
All Please, hurry!
Prince This is like a bad farce!

Amélie and the Prince disappear into the dressing-room

Pochet You see what you're doing to us!
Marcel Let's talk about this later! (*He pushes Pochet off*) Quickly!

Pochet exits into the dressing-room as . . .

Charlotte and Van Putzeboum enter

Van Putzeboum Where is everyone?
Charlotte They were all here just now.
Van Putzeboum Well they aren't now.
Charlotte (*going towards the dressing-room*) I'll see if they're in here.

There is a ring at the doorbell

Oh that's the bell.

She exits

Van Putzeboum So answer! I suppose he's got his financée in a clinch! A man
of passion is my little godsonny.
Étienne (*off*) No, no, don't bother to announce me!
Charlotte (*off*) But monsieur!
Van Putzeboum I know that voice.

Étienne enters

Étienne Good-afternoon Marcel! Oh I beg your pardon!
Van Putzeboum Goodbye, Monsieur Chopart!
Étienne What! Oh yes!
Van Putzeboum I thought you were militating?
Étienne I'm free. Thanks to mumps.
Van Putzeboum Good heavens!
Étienne Blessed illness!
Van Putzeboum And you've come to see your future cousin?
Étienne My future . . .? Yes! Isn't he at home?
Van Putzeboum You should have told him you were coming.
Étienne But what about you? Amélie wrote to tell me you'd returned to
Holland.
Van Putzeboum Yes I did. But now I didn't.
Étienne Oh?
Van Putzeboum I had to rearrange myself. But now I am present at his
wedding.
Étienne What?
Van Putzeboum In memory of his farter.

Étienne (*aside*) Oh my godfathers! (*To Van Putzeboum*) Is Marcel pleased?

Van Putzeboum He made great motions.

Étienne (*aside*) What a mess!

Van Putzeboum The wedding is set for three days' time.

Étienne Really?

Van Putzeboum Yes. And not a moment too soon if you ask me. You see . they're——

Étienne They're what?

Van Putzeboum No I shouldn't really.

Étienne What shouldn't you?

Van Putzeboum I shouldn't tell you. He made me promise not to tell a soul.

Étienne Go on. You can tell me.

Van Putzeboum Of course I can. You're his best friend after all. He'll tell you himself anyway, I'm sure.

Étienne Of course he will, but go on!

Van Putzeboum All right! But only if you promise not to tell anyone else.

Étienne Of course I won't! Now go on!

Van Putzeboum Because you understand that I wouldn't like to undermine Marcel.

Étienne Yes! Yes!

Van Putzeboum Well just between you and me, I think it's high time they got married.

Étienne Why?

Van Putzeboum Because I don't think he can wait any longer. Nor the little ladle. In fact I think the turtledoves are already thinking about laying eggs.

Étienne What do you mean?

Van Putzeboum I found them in bed together earlier today!

Étienne In bed?

Van Putzeboum Yes. She's quite something, isn't she?

Étienne Ooh!

Van Putzeboum What's the matter?

Étienne (*seizing the other by the throat*) You found them in bed together? In bed together?

Van Putzeboum Let me go!

Étienne In bed——

Van Putzeboum What is it to you?

Étienne The dirty swine!

Van Putzeboum But they're going to get married! What does one little indiscretion matter?

Étienne When I think that I trusted him.

Van Putzeboum Gotferdom! I didn't think you'd react like this!

Étienne And this is the man who I called my best friend!

Van Putzeboum Chopart. My dear Chopart, don't take on so.

Étienne Oh leave me alone with your Chopart! There isn't any Chopart! The pigs! The ferret! The swine! (*He stabs at the bed with his rapier*)

Van Putzeboum You gave me your word, Chopart. You owe that to me Gotferdam! Anyway perhaps they were in bed together simply because they were tired.

Étienne Married! Married! Just a minute! Yes, of course . . .

There is a pause while Étienne is buried in thought

Van Putzeboum Chopart! Come on now! Say something.

Étienne I made you a promise and I'll keep it. I shan't say a word to anyone.

Van Putzeboum Thank God for that!

Étienne Besides, perhaps it's like you said. They might simply have been tired.

Van Putzeboum Absolutely!

Étienne Poor young things!

Van Putzeboum (*wiping his brow*) For a moment I have great heat.

Étienne (*aside*) I'll make them pay for this! (*He punctuates this remark with a threatening gesture from his rapier*)

Van Putzeboum (*aside*) Lucky he swallowed that one!

Marcel enters

Marcel Godfather!

Van Putzeboum Ah, here he is!

Marcel (*aside*) My God! Étienne! It's you. Here!

Étienne Yes, here I am!

Amélie enters

Amélie Étienne!

Pochet enters

Pochet You!

Étienne Me!

Amélie (*embracing him*) My dear Étienne!

Étienne My little Amélie. (*He kisses her. To Marcel*) And my good friend Marcel!

Marcel How are you?

Étienne Not bad!

Marcel I'm so pleased to see you!

Étienne Me too!

Pochet You're glad to see each other?

Étienne I'm in seventh heaven!

Marcel (*to Van Putzeboum*) Not a word to him, do you understand? Not a word.

Van Putzeboum (*to Marcel*) What on earth do you think I am?

Marcel (*to Van Putzeboum*) Well . . .

Van Putzeboum (*to Marcel*) You think I'm stupid enough to tell him. You give me a minority complex.

Étienne I hope Amélie's been well behaved.

Marcel Impeccable!

Pochet They've spent all their time together.

Étienne Really?

Pochet They didn't leave each other's side for a moment.

Étienne Well I never! What good friends!

Van Putzeboum Listen children, I came back to fetch you but I see that
Marcel's still not dressed.

Marcel I'm sorry! People keep dropping in.

Van Putzeboum There's no hurry. Besides I'm sure Amélie would like
to spend some time with her cousin as she hasn't seen him for a
fortnight.

Amélie Of course I would.

Van Putzeboum In the meantime I have so much of to do . . . I'll see you
again at Amélie's house in half an hour or so. All right?

All (*in their desire to be rid of him*) Fine, fine.

Van Putzeboum You don't need to see me out. (*To Marcel*) You get dressed.
You shut up. And you others have a good chat. Hallo!

Van Putzeboum exits

All Hallo!

Marcel (*to Étienne*) What an old bore!

Amélie He'll be back soon!

Étienne What's he doing here?

Amélie He's come back for our wedding.

Pochet And he's going to be present at the ceremony.

Étienne Good God! You poor thing. (*To Marcel*) So the game's up?

Marcel Unless there's a miracle . . .

Pochet Not this side of the altar.

Étienne Come on now! Don't let him get your spirits down! There must be a
solution! We've got to make the miracle happen.

Marcel But how can we?

Amélie Yes, how?

Étienne I don't know, but it would never do to leave a dear friend like you in
this mess. (*He grasps Marcel's hand making him cry out in pain*)

Marcel Aaaaah.

Étienne There's only one thing for it. If he wants a wedding then we'll give
him a wedding!

Marcel What do you mean? Do you want me to marry Amélie?

Amélie You want me to marry Marcel?

Marcel It's not that I don't like her, but marriage is a different matter.

Étienne You're right, and besides how could I think of giving my Amélie to
you and her so virtuous, so upright, so faithful! (*He gives her a kiss on every
adjective*)

Amélie Oh please don't! Don't!

Marcel Yes, please don't!

Étienne No it has to be said! Anyway we're doing it to con your godfather
and that's just what we'll do. Now this is what I suggest.

All What?

Étienne We'll go to the Town Hall with Putzeboum and we'll make him take
part in the ceremony: first we'll publish the banns.

Marcel For real?

Étienne For real!

Amélie But that means a real wedding!

Étienne No . . . we'll follow all the formalities of the ceremony but it won't be real in any other sense. Your godfather will be convinced: from then on it's in the bag!

Amélie ⎫
Marcel ⎭ (*together; not understanding*) Yes?

Pochet I'm amazed!

Amélie ⎫
Marcel ⎭ (*together*) Why?

Pochet It's a brilliant idea.

Marcel If you say so.

Amélie Papa?

Marcel Well let us all in on it then.

Étienne I'll hire the room on the appointed day at the Town Hall. I'll take along a friend, from the Stock Exchange: Toto Bejard for example.

Marcel Toto Bejard?

Étienne Yes, you don't know him. (*To Amélie and Pochet*) Nor you.

Pochet I know Chaminet at the Stock Exchange.

Étienne Yes well it's not him. I'll tell Toto, who's a great practical joker . . . I'll tell him to pretend to be the mayor, and then in front of your godforsaken godfather we can celebrate your marriage to Mademoiselle Amélie d'Avranches.

All Bravo! Bravo!

Marcel, Amélie and Pochet form a ring round Étienne and dance

Étienne Yes my friends. Dance! Dance away!

Marcel (*shaking Étienne's hand effusively*) Étienne, you've saved my life! What a friend! What a dear kind friend!

Étienne Just the kind you deserve!

Marcel How can I begin to thank you?

Étienne Don't worry. You can thank me later.

They dance as —

—*the* CURTAIN *falls*

ACT III

SCENE 1

The wedding parlour at the Town Hall

Mouilletu (*to Yvonne*) Not on the chairs. The chairs are reserved for the bridal party.

Yvonne Sorry, I didn't realize.

Valcreuse and Boas enter arm-in-arm talking loudly

Boas Well my dear, they caught him cheating and out he went.

Valcreuse What a story!

Boas Usher! Where's the Courbois wedding?

Mouilletu Here monsieur!

Yvonne Psst. Over here!

Valcreuse Look! It's Yvonne!

Boas Yvonne! There you are!

Yvonne Here I am!

Valcreuse is about to sit on a chair

Mouilletu Not on the chairs! Benches only please!

Valcreuse (*ironically*) Thank you very much!

Boas Hallo Yvonne.

Valcreuse You all right?

Yvonne Bonjour, mes enfants; you don't want to miss the show, eh?

Boas You're telling me!

Valcreuse What show?

Yvonne Come off it! It's the hottest ticket in town!

Boas It's incredible.

Yvonne What?

Boas This wedding!

Valcreuse Marcel marrying Amélie.

Yvonne It's only a joke.

Boas Not any more; the wedding's really taking place.

Yvonne No listen! Marcel spent last night at Tabarin's and he assured us all that it was a practical joke to fool his godfather . . . it's all about an inheritance.

Boas You're the fool, chérie. This is the Town Hall.

Yvonne That's what he told me!

Cornette enters. He has one shoulder higher than the other

Cornette Mouilletu! Mouilletu!

Mouilletu Monsieur Cornette!

Cornette Hallo Mouilletu! The boss hasn't been asking for me, has he?
Mouilletu Yes he has. I said you were already in, don't worry.
Cornette Thanks! I was held up a little longer than anticipated.
Mouilletu At the café, I suppose?
Cornette I was playing a hand of poker with Jobinet.
Mouilletu Jobinet?
Cornette The one with a million jokes. You know him; he works for the undertaker.
Mouilletu Oh yes! I hope you won!
Cornette No chance! Not surprising really! He's a hunchback!

The Mayor puts his head round the door

Mayor Cornette!
Cornette Here, your worship! I'm coming!

Cornette exits after the Mayor

Palmyre enters

Boas Look, there's Palmyre.
Yvonne So it is! (*She signals to them*)
Boas
Valcreuse } (*together*) Hey! Hey!
Palmyre Hallo.
Yvonne Did you stay much later last night?
Palmyre Until six o'clock. We all said we'd meet again here but everybody was so exhausted I expect they've all stayed in bed!
Boas That's where we should be!
Yvonne That'd be nice.
Mouilletu Not on the chairs, madame, not on the chairs.
Yvonne Who does he think he is?
Palmyre I hear that someone called Toto Bejard's taking the part of the Mayor.
Boas
Valcreuse } (*together*) Toto Bejard?
Palmyre He's from the Stock Exchange.
Yvonne (*to Boas*) There, you see! (*To the women*) Didn't Marcel explain that the wedding was a joke to fool his godfather?
Palmyre Yes!
Yvonne Told you!
Boas It's beyond me!

A Photographer enters

Mouilletu (*seeing him*) The wedding procession will come from there, monsieur. (*Taking his card; impressed*) Ah, from *Le Matin*?

Another Photographer enters

(*Taking his card*) From *Le Journal*? Snap!

The Photographers shake hands

Boas (*to Mouilletu*) Usher!
Mouilletu Monsieur?
Boas The wedding is at three, isn't it?
Mouilletu Yes, monsieur.

The Mayor puts his head round the door

Mayor Mouilletu! Mouilletu!
Mouilletu Coming, your worship!

Mouilletu exits after the Mayor

Valcreuse Three minutes to go!
Boas Not long. Good.

The orchestra strikes up the Wedding March

Yvonne The music! We're off!
Palmyre It's the bride and groom! They're arriving!
All The bride and groom!

Mouilletu enters

Mouilletu The procession, ladies and gentlemen! Make way!

He exits

Yvonne Let's see them come in!

Mouilletu comes back in from the atrium

Mouilletu Order ladies and gentlemen! Please! Stand back and make way for
the bridal procession!

*The procession enters, Amélie at its head in her bridal gown with her father on
her arm. He is holding his hat and wears his Palestrian medal around his neck.
Behind him comes Marcel. Adonis follows in a smoking jacket. He is holding
the hand of a six-year-old child who is the maid of honour. She holds a posy of
flowers. They are followed by the witnesses: Étienne, Van Putzeboum,
Koshnadieff and Bibichon*

This way please! This way.
Various voices Doesn't she look lovely! What a nice dress! Doesn't she look
happy! *etc.*

*They process towards the Mayor's desk. The Photographers take snaps. As
Amélie passes various people they compliment her and she answers each one
with a thank you*

Mouilletu Right up here! Thank you ladies and gentlemen.
Amélie Papa, are you crying?
Pochet No! Yes! What do you expect? It's the excitement! They're not
exactly tears. More like peeling an onion!
Amélie I see!
Pochet To see one's only daughter dressed in an orange blossom dress in
front of a crowd like this . . .

Amélie But it's all a joke!

Pochet I know it's a joke but even so! (*He dries his eyes*) Marriage is a fine institution!

Amélie Calm down!

Mouilletu Follow me, ladies and gentlemen.

Pochet Coming! Coming!

Adonis (*dragging the little girl behind him*) Come on you brat! Why do you always have to be dragged?

The Brat 'Cos I do!

Adonis The idea of the concierge's kid as a maid of honour is too ridiculous for words!

Mouilletu The bride here and the groom there please!

Van Putzeboum (*to Étienne*) This is the big day eh? The dear young things, they must be volcanic!

Étienne Oh yes, the dear young things!

Mouilletu The father here and the mother there!

Pochet There is no mother!

Yvonne No, but I'm her best friend!

Mouilletu Witnesses?

Koshnadieff ⎫
Bibichon   ⎭ (*together*) Here!

Mouilletu The bride's witnesses here. The bridegroom's witnesses there.

Koshnadieff It was his Highness's wish that I act as witness.

Bibichon Really? They chose me because I was respectable.

Van Putzeboum (*seeing Adonis and the Brat move into his place*) Oy, you. Get off it!

Yvonne (*to Boas*) Doesn't it make you want to do it yourself?

Boas What! With you?

Yvonne Yes, me!

Boas It had crossed my mind.

Palmyre (*indicating Valcreuse*) If I wanted him to marry, I've only to say the word!

Valcreuse Possibly. But it wouldn't be to you!

Palmyre But you told me only the other day——

Valcreuse The other night don't you mean . . . at night you often say things——

Boas Out of politeness.

Mouilletu The best man and the maid of honour?

The Brat That's us, dearest.

Adonis (*being dragged by her*) Dearest! You pigmy!

Mouilletu Best man here, maid of honour there!

Adonis What time do you go to bed?

The Brat At eight o'clock, young man.

Adonis After you've changed your nappy, eh?

The Brat What?

Adonis Shut up!

Mouilletu (*to the remainder of the guests*) If you would all sit down on these chairs! His worship, the Mayor, will be with you in a moment.

Mouilletu exits

Marcel (*to Étienne*) Tell me . . .
Étienne What?
Marcel Toto Bejard's still playing the Mayor?
Étienne Yes.
Marcel Amélie!
Amélie What?
Marcel Toto Bejard is still playing the Mayor!
Amélie Yes, I know!
Pochet What? What did he say?
Amélie Nothing! He was just saying that Toto Bejard's still playing the Mayor.
Pochet Oh! Yes! (*To Van Putzeboum*) Toto Bejard's the Mayor.
Van Putzeboum What did he say the Mayor was called? Toto Bejard?
Étienne No! Yes! It's not really important.

The four guests suddenly explode with laughter

Yvonne How can you!?
Boas What do you mean? Don't you recognize wit?
Amélie What is it? What's he up to?
Boas (*laughing*) Nothing! Nothing!
Palmyre He was making jokes in rather bad taste.
Amélie Oh go on! Go on!
Valcreuse⎫
Yvonne   ⎬ (*together*) He was asking——
Palmyre ⎭
Yvonne No, you say . . .
Amélie What was he asking?
Pochet Come on now all of you, behave! Where do you think you are, eh?

There is a muted repetition amongst the congregation of "Where do you think you are?"

Mouilletu enters and mounts the podium

The Brat whispers in Adonis's ear

Adonis What? What did you say?

The Brat whispers again

What now? We're just about to get started.
Amélie What's the matter?
Adonis Nothing!
Amélie What is it?
Adonis She . . . (*He goes and speaks privately to Amélie*)
Amélie Well, go on.
Adonis Oh no! It's got nothing to do with me.
Pochet What is going on?
Amélie Nothing Papa. She . . . (*She speaks privately to her father*)

Pochet Ah?
Adonis Exactly.
Pochet Well go on. It's only natural.
Amélie (*to Mouilletu*) Usher!
Mouilletu Mademoiselle?
Amélie Could you tell me where . . . (*She speaks privately to the usher*)
Adonis Charming!
Mouilletu Certainly, mademoiselle. Is it Monsieur (*indicating Adonis*) who
   wants to . . .
Adonis No, it isn't!
Mouilletu It's the little girl, is it? This way, young lady!
The Brat (*dragging Adonis*) Aren't you going to come too?
Adonis Get away from me!
Amélie Go on! Go with her.
Adonis Me?
Pochet The best man never leaves the side of his maid of honour.
Adonis No, I won't go!
Amélie I'm telling you to go . . . you can't let her go on her own.
Adonis (*furious*) Damn!
Pochet We're not asking the impossible!
Adonis What will people think of me?
Mouilletu Please let the maid of honour through! Let the maid of honour
   through!

Everbody moves to create a passage for the Brat

Adonis Why couldn't you go before we came?
Mouilletu This way, this way!
Adonis Wretched brat!

As Mouilletu points the way

   Yes thank you. There's no need to go on pointing, monsieur. I'll find it!
   Come on brat!

They exit

Van Putzeboum Where are they going?
Étienne Nowhere. She . . . (*He whispers into Van Putzeboum's ear*)
Van Putzeboum Like the little statue . . . Psst.
Étienne You said it!
Van Putzeboum (*delighted*) A real Parisian wedding!
Marcel Where is Toto Bejard? I want to get on.
Amélie You're telling me! I'v got to see the Prince at home at four o'clock.
Mouilletu Ladies and gentlemen, his worship the Mayor!

The Mayor, in full regalia enters followed by Cornette

The assembly rises and at a gesture from the Mayor sits down again

Mayor (*signalling to Pochet to be seated*) Monsieur!
Amélie Papa!

Pochet Sorry! (*Thinking that the Mayor wants to shake his hand*) Pleased to meet you.

Mayor I was asking you to sit down.

Pochet Sorry!

Marcel (*to Étienne*) Is that really Toto Bejard?

Étienne Yes!

Mayor Is anything the matter?

Marcel No nothing. (*To Étienne*) He looks just right! You're sure he's not going to let us down.

Étienne He'll play his part all right.

Mayor (*asking for silence*) Please! (*To Marcel*) The bridegroom?

Amélie (*nudging Marcel*) Marcel!

Marcel What? Me?

Mayor I think there's only one, monsieur. Can I have your Christian and surnames please?

Marcel (*to Étienne*) He's splendid!

Étienne Isn't he!

Marcel (*stifling laughter*) Joseph-Marcel Courbois.

Mayor Why are you laughing?

Marcel No reason, your worship.

Mayor And you mademoiselle?

Pochet Clementine-Amélie Pochet.

Mayor Not you. I was asking Mademoiselle here.

Pochet Sorry!

Amélie Clementine-Amélie Pochet.

Pochet (*to the Mayor*) That's what I said.

Mayor So you did.

Pochet I'm her father, you know. I gave her her names. I knew them before she did, in fact!

Mayor Please monsieur, may we continue?

Pochet Continue, your worship. Continue.

Van Putzeboum (*to Étienne*) Pochet? I thought her name was d'Avranches.

Étienne Yes . . . well . . . that was a title given her by the Pope. It's not used at official ceremonies.

Van Putzeboum Good heavens.

Mayor You will now be read the act of marriage. Cornette!

Marcel Toto Bejard is amazing, you'd think he'd been doing it all his life.

Cornette (*resting his head in his hands while he reads*) On the fifth of May nineteen hundred and eight, the Mayor of the eighteenth Arrondissement of Paris has before him to be wedded in matrimony Monsieur Joseph Marcel Courbois a bachelor and a private gentleman living at twenty-seven Rue Cambon . . . (*His voice drones on in the background as the following takes place*)

Amélie Marcel! Have you seen his lump?

Marcel What lump?

Amélie The Mayor's lump!

Marcel My word yes!

Amélie Have you seen his lump, Papa?

Pochet What!
Amélie The Mayor's lump!
Pochet It's quite a lump!
Amélie It's as big as a egg.
Marcel (*to Étienne*) You didn't tell me that Toto Bejard had a lump.
Étienne Quiet! It's not a real one. It's part of his disguise.
Marcel Really. (*To Amélie*) The Mayor's lump is false.
Amélie Really. (*To Pochet*) Papa! It's false!
Pochet Really. (*Getting up*) Amazing! (*He takes a pair of spectacles from his pocket and fixing them on his nose advances towards the Mayor to get a better look*)
Mayor Whatever is it now?
Pochet (*giving him a look as if to say "Come off it"*) Nothing. Nothing at all your worship! (*As he takes his seat, to Amélie*) I'd swear it was real, myself.
Yvonne (*to Pochet*) What would you swear was real?
Pochet The Mayor's lump. It's false.
Yvonne Really? (*To her neighbours*) Did you know the Mayor's lump is false?
Koshnadieff (*indifferent*) Ah?
Palmyre What did you say was false?
Pochet The Mayor's lump.

All the occupants of the second row in which Palmyre is seated say "Impossible!"

Yvonne (*passing on the news to the third row*) The Mayor's lump is false.
Third row No!
Second row Yes!
One or two occupants of the fourth row What's false? What did she say?
Third row The Mayor's lump is false!
Somebody from the fourth row His lump? Oh!

The occupants of the first row, apart from Van Putzeboum who is asleep and Étienne, get up and close in on the Mayor to try to look more closely at the lump: the second row follow suit when the Mayor suddenly looks up and all retreat to their places

Mayor Now what is it? What on earth's the matter?
All Nothing! Nothing!

Koshnadieff remains standing

Mayor What is wrong with you?
Koshnadieff Apparently it's false.
Mayor What is?
Koshnadieff I don't know.
Mayor (*to Mouilletu*) My God, what a wedding!
Cornette (*now getting louder*) . . . have publicly announced that Joseph-Marcel Courbois and Clementine-Amélie Pochet are united as man and wife.   *
Koshnadieff Bravo! Slavenska.
Mayor Chut! (*To Pochet*) Stand up!

Pochet, Amélie and Marcel all stand

(*To Marcel and Amélie*) Sit down!

All sit

(*To Pochet*) No, stand up! Sit down. Stand up.

Marcel Are we supposed to be standing or sitting?

Mayor (*to Marcel*) I was addressing Monsieur Pochet! Sit down! (*To Pochet*) Why are you sitting down?

Pochet You just said, I was addressing Monsieur Pochet, sit down.

Mayor Let's get it straight, shall we? I was addressing Monsieur Pochet. Sit down bride and groom and you Monsieur Pochet, on your feet.

Pochet Got it!

Marcel Well he only had to say!

Mayor (*to Pochet*) Monsieur Alphonse Amedee Pochet!

Pochet That's me.

Mayor I know it is. Do you consent to the marriage of your daughter Clementine-Amélie Pochet to Joseph-Marcel Courbois?

Pochet With joy!

Mayor Don't say "with joy"!

Pochet I say what I feel.

Mayor I've noticed, but please keep your intimate feelings to yourself. Just say, "yes" or "no".

Pochet Absolutely.

Mayor No, not "absolutely". Yes or no.

Pochet Yes, of course. Why else would I have come here?

Mayor Good! Now, I turn once more——

At this moment Adonis and the Brat enter

They are welcomed by the crowd with an "Ahhhhh!" which interrupts the Mayor

Amélie Done!

Adonis You wait!

Pochet He'd find her charming if she were ten years older.

Mayor I turn once more——

Bibichon Five would do for me!

Koshnadieff (*laughing*) Ho, ho, ho!

All join in general conversation

Mayor When you've all finished!

Bibichon Sorry!

Pochet Please! We're at the Town Hall!

Mayor I'm glad you remembered.

Pochet (*repeating to everybody*) I'm glad too.

Mayor (*to Pochet*) Will you be quiet!

Pochet (*and emphasizing every syllable*) Will you be quiet! (*To the Mayor*) There, your worship!

Mayor Shut up!

Pochet Of course.

Marcel He's capital this Toto Bejard. Such natural authority!
Mayor And now I turn once more to the bride and groom.
Pochet (*turning to the assembled company*) Listen!
Mayor Silence!
Pochet (*repeating to everybody*) Silence!
Mayor (*to Pochet*) Silence!
Pochet I've just told them. (*Repeating to everybody*) Silence!
Mayor You!
Pochet Oh me! (*To himself*) Silence!
Van Putzeboum What a chatter chest!

Irene enters the vestibule. She speaks to one of the photographers

Irene Is this the wedding?
Mayor (*to Marcel and Amélie*) Now! Are you both ready?
Marcel ⎫
          ⎬ (*together*) Yes, your worship.
Amélie ⎭
Mayor Monsieur Joseph Marcel Courbois!
Marcel Here I am your worship.
Amélie (*seeing Irene*) Madame!
Mayor Do you take this woman for your wife——
Amélie (*to Marcel*) Look Marcel, it's Madame, over there!
Mayor Mademoiselle Clementine.
Marcel Who? Irene!
Mayor Amélie!
Amélie Yes!
Mayor Pochet?
Marcel (*surprised at seeing Irene*) No!
Mayor No! What do you mean "no"?
Marcel What? Oh that. Well, of course . . .
Mayor What do you mean, "of course". Yes or no.
Marcel Yes. (*To Irene*) Hallo, hallo!
Mayor Mademoiselle Clementine-Amélie Pochet!
Amélie (*to Marcel*) It's so nice of her to have come.
Mayor Mademoiselle Clementine . . . Clementine! Amélie! Mademoiselle Pochet!
Pochet Amélie!
Amélie Here I am! Here I am!
Mayor (*to Mouilletu*) What is the matter with this lot?
Pochet Pay attention!
Amélie Yes, yes. (*To Pochet*) It's because Madame la Comtesse de Premilly's here. There, at the back.
Pochet Madame? No? Has she come? So she has! (*He waves*) Madame! Hallo, madame!
Mayor Mademiselle Pochet, do you want to be married today?
Amélie Yes, your worship! Sorry, your worship! (*Pointing to Irene*) It's because Madame's come along . . .
Mayor Fine. Mademoiselle Clementine-Amélie Pochet, do you take Monsieur Marcel Courbois as your husband?

Amélie Well that speaks for itself!

Mayor Is that supposed to be an answer?

Amélie Sorry! Yes, your worship. Yes!

Mayor In the name of the law, I declare Monsieur Joseph-Marcel Courbois and Mademoiselle Clementine-Amélie Pochet are united as man and wife.

Koshnadieff Bravo!

All Bravo!

Mayor Messieurs! Messieurs! We're not at the theatre!

Étienne (*aside*) Done it!

Marcel What did you say?

Étienne What? Nothing? I just said, done it.

Marcel Yes, we've done it. (*To Amélie*) We've done it! (*To Irene*) We've done it!

Mouilletu If you would sign the register Monsieur and Madame Courbois? And the relatives and witnesses?

All the first row get up and go to Cornette's table to sign the register, except Amélie and Pochet who go to Mouilletu's table. Adonis goes and sits in Van Putzeboum's chair and the Brat goes and sits on Palmyre's lap

Mayor (*to Amélie*) If you'll just sign there, mademoiselle! (*After she has signed*) Thank you, madame! (*To Marcel*) Your friends are insane, monsieur!

Marcel I'm sorry but they didn't know how seriously to take you.

Mayor What?

Marcel You did very well, Toto. Very well!

Mayor Toto? What do you mean Toto?

Marcel (*putting his finger to his mouth and pointing to Van Putzeboum*) Shhh! The godfather! Shhh!

Mayor I don't understand a word you're saying.

Marcel Oh very good!

Mayor What do you mean, "the godfather"?

Van Putzeboum Did you call me?

Marcel No, not us!

Mayor (*aside*) They're all peasants!

Marcel (*to Étienne*) Your Toto Bejard's a lad. He wouldn't give the game away, not even to me.

Étienne I told you, he'd lie to his grandmother.

Mouilletu If the married couple would step forward to receive the Mayor's congratulations.

Everyone goes back to their place

Mayor Monsieur and Madame Courbois . . .!

Marcel No jokes, eh?

Mayor (*loudly*) What?

Marcel Nothing, nothing. If that's how you want to play it, it's fine with me.

Mayor Monsieur and Madame Courbois, despite the fact that I have singularly failed to discover in either you or your (*he looks at the assembly*) friends an ounce of the seriousness which I normally expect to find displayed on such occasions that will not prevent me from pursuing the traditional practice. And so without further ado, I would ask both Monsieur and Madame Courbois——

Koshnadieff Bravo!

Mayor —to accept the most sincere best wishes of the Mayor for your future happiness together.

All Bravo!

Amélie Thank you very much your worship.

Marcel Me too. (*Leaning towards him*) When I said "It's the godfather", it was because it's him we're playing the trick on.

Mayor I see. (*After a pause*) What trick?

Marcel What an actor! (*He playfully hits the Mayor in the stomach*)

Mayor Ow!

Amélie And that lump's really too much! (*She pretends to tweak the Mayor's lump*)

Mayor (*outraged*) Madame, that's enough! (*Aside*) They're driving me mad! Mesdames . . . messieurs, good-day to you.

He exits, followed by Cornette

Mouilletu Ladies and gentlemen the ceremony is concluded.

The band strikes up the Wedding March

Marcel Let's go. Amélie! Watch out for your train.

Amélie (*to Pochet*) Papa, watch where you put your feet!

Pochet Don't worry! I'll keep my distance.

Amélie (*to Adonis after she has kissed the Brat*) Take good care of her! If she needs the——

Adonis Oh no! I'm not looking after her.

They begin to process out of the parlour. The guests file past the couple offering a variety of comments and compliments and Pochet in turn invites each one to the wedding breakfast at Gilet's

When the guests have left, Marcel, Étienne, Amélie, Pochet and Irene are left. Mouilletu is at his desk looking after the registers

Irene Hallo Marcel!

Marcel There you are!

Irene I wouldn't have missed seeing that!

Amélie Good-afternoon Madame la Comtesse. I hope you're well? Papa, it's Madame.

Pochet I do hope you'll be able to come to the wedding breakfast, madame?

Irene Thank you Pochet, but really I couldn't.

Pochet But it's at Gilet's. Surely you won't turn down my little offering? It's only a glass of Madeira and a biscuit.

Irene Thank you Pochet, but no.

Pochet I'm deeply saddened.

Irene I'm sorry dear Pochet.

Marcel You saw it all, did you? When we were joined together?

Irene I got here for that; it was very funny.
Marcel Hilarious!
Irene But it did work? Your godfather was taken in?
Marcel And how!
Pochet He was so attentive you could have heard a pin drop.
Irene No more problems, no worries?
Marcel Not a care in the world!

Étienne laughs to himself

   What's he laughing about?
Irene You're a rich man at last.
Marcel Oh my dear little Rene. (*He tries to kiss her*)
Irene Marcel!
Marcel What's the matter? You're allowed to kiss the bridegroom.
Irene Of course.

She and Marcel kiss

Amélie Watch out! Here's your godfather.
Marcel Oh!
Irene I'll wait for you in the vestibule.

   Irene exits

   Van Putzeboum enters and watches Irene's departure

Van Putzeboum Who was that?
Marcel Nobody! A country relation.
Pochet She was his wet nurse.
Van Putzeboum They start young in the country!
Marcel Don't they?
Van Putzeboum But that's enough of that, little godsonny. I wanted to pay
   you my own compliments on your marriage.
Marcel ⎱ (*together*) Thank you, Godfather.
Amélie ⎰
Pochet You will come to the breakfast, won't you?
Van Putzeboum Thank you for your unforgettable hostility. And the happy
   couple? You're coming, aren't you?
Marcel Oh no! The bride and groom never appear at the wedding breakfast.
   They go home together . . . you do understand, don't you?
Van Putzeboum Perfectly! But before you go, you will allow me one little
   smack, won't you?
Marcel (*pushing Van Putzeboum towards Amélie*) Smack away, Godfather,
   smack away!
Pochet You're over-generous with your smack, always.
Mouilletu (*coming to join them*) Here is your marriage certificate.
Marcel (*snatching it and waving it under Étienne's nose*) My certificate! My
   certificate! (*To Mouilletu, tipping him*) Thank you, my man.
Mouilletu Thank you, monsieur. All the very best to you.
Marcel Étienne: You've thought of everything.
Étienne Yes, everything!

Van Putzeboum What do you mean, everything?
Marcel Well he's . . . been so very thoughtful . . .

Kashnadieff arrives with Amélie's coat which he puts over her shoulders

Koshnadieff Madame, if you are ready?
Amélie Yes of course. (*To Marcel*) Listen, I'm going off with the General. The Prince is waiting for me.
Marcel Oh yes!
Amélie If my husband will allow?
Marcel What?
Amélie We're a married couple now, chéri. Shall we go, General?
Koshnadieff I am at your service, madame.
Van Putzeboum You aren't leaving?
Amélie Yes.

Amélie and Koshnadieff exit

Marcel She's going on ahead. I'm joining her later.
Van Putzeboum I'd better go and look for my cͻat then. Now that you've fulfilled the condition of your father's will, I'll go to the hotel and bring you your cheque. Hallo.
Marcel (*pushing him out*) Good idea! Hallo!
Pochet As everyone else is off, I'd better go too.
Marcel (*pushing him out*) Good idea!

Van Putzeboum exits

Pochet I'll see you at Gilet's then?
Marcel No, I'm not going. But have a good meal!
Pochet Thanks.

Pochet exits

Marcel Yippee!
Étienne Yippee!
Marcel Did it!
Étienne Did it!
Marcel (*like old fellow sportsmen*) Hon.
Étienne Hon, hon.
Marcel Hon, hon, hon.
Marcel
Étienne (*together*) Hon, hon, hon, hon, hon, hon.
Marcel Thank you so much, old pal! Thank you.
Étienne You're pleased, eh?
Marcel Pleased? Delighted! Can you believe it? They fell for it.
Étienne They fell for it.
Marcel And my godfather! He was certainly taken in. What a joke, what a wonderful joke!
Étienne Wonderful! In fact even better than you can begin to imagine.
Marcel It couldn't be!
Étienne It could!

Marcel (*like old fellow sportsmen*) Hon!
Étienne Hon, hon.
Marcel Hon, hon, hon.
Marcel
Étienne   (*together*) Hon, hon, hon, hon, hon, hon.
Étienne The best joke was making you believe the marriage wasn't for real.
Marcel What?
Étienne You thought that it was all a joke, didn't you? Well, mon vieux, it wasn't!
Marcel What! Do you mean——
Étienne You took my mistress from me and went to bed with her.
Marcel But, but . . . then you know?
Étienne Yes, I know.
Marcel Ouch!
Étienne Anyway, old pal, do it again if you want to. There's nothing to be ashamed of. She's your wife now! You've just married her!
Marcel What are you saying?
Étienne Goodbye! Have fun! Oh . . . and remember "Keep an eye on Amélie." (*He starts to exit*)
Marcel Étienne! Étienne!
Étienne (*his voice floating back*) "Keep an eye on Amélie".

Étienne exits

Marcel Étienne! Étienne! Come back . . .

The Mayor enters

Ah! Toto, a minute please! Come here ! Quickly! (*He seizes the Mayor by the collar*)
Mayor What is the meaning of this?
Marcel What really happened in here just now?
Mayor What do you mean, "really"?
Marcel The wedding. Was it for real? Did you really marry me to Amélie?
Mayor Of course it was for real!
Marcel No, no. Don't say it.
Mayor What in heaven's name did you think you'd come here to do?
Marcel You mean I've married . . . But I didn't want to! I want a divorce!
Mayor (*going*) That's not my job.
Marcel Then you're not Toto Bejard?
Mayor I am the Mayor of this district.
Marcel The Mayor of this dis—aaaah! (*He falls into the Mayor's arms*)
Mayor Come now! Come now!

Irene enters

Irene Marcel! What's the matter?
Marcel Irene! I've just married Amélie!
Irene What do you mean?
Mayor (*still holding Marcel*) Please monsieur!
Marcel Étienne has tricked us. I am married to Amélie d'Avranches!

Irene You're married to—aaaah! (*She faints into the Mayor's arms*)
Mayor Oh my God! Her too! Help! Somebody! Mouilletu! Cornette! Help!

Everybody rushes in on the Mayor's cry for help

All What's happened? What's the matter?
Marcel I've married Amélie!
All What!
Marcel I've married Amélie d'Avranches!
Bibichon What are you talking about?
Van Putzeboum What is the matter, little godsonny?
Marcel Godfather! I've married Amélie d'Avranches!
Van Putzeboum Yes? I know you have, isn't it wonderful.
Bibichon Good Lord! I signed the register!
Marcel I have married Amélie d'Avranches!

CURTAIN

SCENE 2

Amélie's bedroom

The Prince is discovered in his underpants pacing up and down the room

Prince My God, what is she doing? I never thought it took so long to get married!

The doorbell rings

Someone at the door.

The door opens and the General appears on his own

Well? Where is she?
Koshnadieff The bride has arrived, sir.
Prince At last!
Koshnadieff Mademoiselle d'Avranches, if you'd be so kind . . .

Amélie enters

Amélie Sir, I am so very sorry, if—oh!
Prince What is it?
Amélie Nothing. Just your dress, sir. I wasn't expecting—
Prince It's to save time. Leave us Koshnadieff!
Koshnadieff Yes sir.

He exits

Amélie I thought your Highness might come to fetch me . . . but I didn't think you intended to, you know . . . here!
Prince Why not? It's very nice here. Everyone's out.
Amélie Yes, of course. But propriety . . .

Prince Princes decide propriety, my dear. You've kept me waiting for eternity . . . Take off your frock!

Amélie What now? Already?

Prince Newly-weds are always impatient. (*He stretches to grab her*)

Amélie Oh sir! I must take off my veil.

Prince If you knew how impatient I've been.

Amélie Oh, my hair's such a mess.

Prince You're adorable. Let your hair fall on your shoulders.

Amélie What?

Prince Like a mane! I love to run my bare feet over the tossing mane of my lover.

Amélie How very refined! But very unusual here in Paris.

Prince (*seeing her undo her dress*) Please let me help you.

Amélie Thank you, sir. It's so hard on one's own.

Prince (*undoing her dress*) Oh this is exciting. The first night of one's honeymoon.

Amélie By proxy!

Prince Droit de seigneur! Very Louis Quatorze! Did it go well?

Amélie What?

Prince Your wedding with the landlord?

Amélie I told you before, he's not the landlord!

Amélie Yes, yes, I know. But to me he'll always be the landlord. Did your trick work? Did the godfather fall for it?

Amélie Like Adam!

Prince Bravo! I love jokes and I was very pleased to be able to order the General to be of service to you.

Amélie We were very honoured.

Prince Good.

Amélie has now taken off her dress. The Prince picks it up and throws it on the sofa

Was he all right?

Amélie Who?

Prince The General.

Amélie Wonderful!

Prince That doesn't surprise me. I'm told he's good at weddings. I wonder what he'd be like in a war. (*Looking at Amélie half-naked*) Dear God! (*He kisses her on the neck*) Ah!

Amélie Oh sir! You're tickling me!

Prince And you me!

Amélie Me sir?

Prince What do you like?

Amélie I've heard that before!

The doorbell rings

Prince What's that?

Amélie There's somebody at the door.

Prince Who is it?

Amélie I don't know. But the kitchen maid'll deal with them.

Prince Good.

Marcel (*off*) Amélie! Amélie!

Prince ⎱ (*together*) Don't come in!
Amélie ⎰

   Marcel enters

Marcel Amélie! Amélie!

Amélie You?

Prince The landlord!

Marcel What?

Prince Aren't you the happy man!

Marcel Happy! Oh Amélie! The whole pack of cards has collapsed.

Amélie What is it?

Marcel We're married. You and I are legally man and wife!

Prince What?

Amélie What are you talking about?

Marcel Toto Bejard wasn't Toto Bejard at all. It was the Mayor!

Amélie Don't be silly! What on earth do you mean?

Marcel Étienne knew everything. He knew that we'd been to bed . . .

Amélie No!

Marcel Yes!

Amélie Oh my God!

Marcel This was his revenge. The bastard! My best friend! He had us married! We really are man and wife!

Amélie What? Both of us?

Marcel Both of us! I'm your husband and you're my wife!

Amélie But then . . . I'm Madame Courbois!

Marcel Yes.

Amélie Chéri! How lovely! (*She puts her arms around Marcel and kisses him*)

Marcel What?

Prince Monsieur, my congratulations. I wish you all the very best.

Amélie (*presenting Marcel to the Prince*) My husband. (*To herself, quite liking the idea*) My husband! (*To the Prince*) His Highness, the Prince of Palestrie.

Marcel What?

Prince Delighted to meet you, monsieur.

Marcel I'm going mad!

Amélie You'll see what a wife you've married. Domesticated, faithful . . .

Prince Faithful?

Marcel What do you mean "faithful"!

Amélie Oh yes. I am half-naked at the moment but, well . . . you'll see! (*She goes to the bed and puts on a dressing-gown*)

Prince Forgive her, Monsieur Amélie.

Marcel What's he calling me?

Prince (*to Amélie*) Shall I help you on with your kimono?

Amélie Thank you sir. And now, I'm afraid I really must ask you to leave.

Prince Pardon?

Amélie I'm sorry, but in view of the circumstances . . .

Prince But . . . but . . . but . . . I came for . . . (*He points to the bed*)

Amélie (*mock outrage*) Really, sir!

Prince Well this is all very unfortunate! I don't really see why . . . I mean it was agreed that——

Amélie Please, sir! This is my husband!

Marcel Ah!

Prince You're right, I will take my leave, of course. It's quite clear that you . . . I mean that . . . believe me monsieur, I didn't come here for . . . for . . . oh! (*He takes his hat, coat, cane and putting on his gloves, bows to Amélie*) Madame, I offer you my deepest respects.

Amélie Sir.

Forgetting that he is dressed only in his underpants, the Prince puts his hat on and tries to leave. Marcel bars his way

Marcel Oh no. Do you think I'm going to let matters stay as they are? Do you think I'm going to accept this marriage lying down?

Amélie What's done is done!

Marcel Then it can be undone! I want a divorce!

The Prince puts down his gloves and cane but keeps his hat on throughout the scene

Amélie Divorce?

Marcel Exactly!

Amélie Oh no! No, no, no, no, no! I am against divorce and so is Papa!

Marcel I don't care. I was forced into marrying you. It's null and void.

Amélie You can't mean that?

Marcel The law is quite precise in the matter. The union is invalid if both parties don't consent to it.

Amélie But you did consent. You said "yes".

Marcel That's because I was taken in.

Amélie Possibly. But all the same you did say "yes" and that's a fact.

Marcel I can't bear it!

Prince Now, listen here landlord!

Marcel Oh, why don't you go away!

Prince I beg your pardon? I'll have you know that I am the Prince of Palestrie!

Marcel Well, this isn't Palestrie! It's the home of Amélie D'Avranches and I'm her husband.

Amélie But it's just because you're my husband—

Marcel A woman whose lovers are the talk of Paris!

Amélie Really!

Marcel A woman who spends her wedding night with the Prince of Palestrie.

Prince Nothing happened!

Marcel And this is the woman to whom I've given my good name!

Amélie Now that's quite enough unless you want me to really do something.

Marcel What?

Amélie (*putting her hand on the Prince's shoulder*) The Prince is still here don't forget.

Prince Me?

Marcel The Prince! Of course! Don't worry, I'll really do something. Probably couldn't have a better opportunity. (*He runs to the window and opens it*)

Prince What's he doing?

Amélie What are you going to do?

Prince (*seizing Marcel*) Unhappy man!

Marcel Let me go!

Prince You're not going to throw yourself out of the window?

Marcel Not me!

Prince (*letting go of him*) What then?

Amélie Who?

Prince Not us?

Marcel No! These! (*He picks up the Prince's clothes from the bed and throws them out of the window*)

Prince ⎱ (*together*) Aahh!
Amélie ⎰

Marcel runs to the door and exits

Prince My clothes! He's thrown my clothes out of the window!

Amélie Marcel! Marcel!

Prince Landlord! Landlord!

Both arrive at the door and find it locked

Amélie He's locked us in!

Prince How dare he lock up the Prince of Palestrie!

Amélie The beast!

Prince (*running to the dressing-room*) Through here?

Amélie That's my dressing-room. There's no way out of it.

Prince In Palestrie he'd be flogged in public and sent to the galleys.

Amélie Not in France! (*She goes to the window*)

Prince But good Lord, I can't stay locked in here without any clothes!

Amélie It's him! Marcel! Marcel!

Prince You've seen him?

Amélie Yes, he's going into the Police Station on the other side of the street.

Prince The Police Station?

Amélie What's he up to?

Prince If he brings the police here I'll have him arrested! For daring to lock up the Prince of Palestrie.

Amélie Be careful, sir! Remember, he is my husband.

Prince So what? He ambushed me.

Amélie He'll tell them he caught us *in flagrante delicto*.

Prince What a terrible scandal. Think of my government! Is there no other way out?

Amélie Only the window.

Prince We're on the second floor!

Amélie The pavement's quite soft!
Prince You could wave at people in the street. Attract their attention.
Amélie Opposite the Police Station! No thank you!
Prince Well what then?
Amélie We'll just have to stay here.
Prince (*in despair*) Oh!

There is a noise of voices outside

Amélie Listen!
Prince What is it?
Amélie He's coming back!
Prince Ah!
Amélie But not alone! There's somebody with him!
Prince Oh!

He exits into the dressing-room as . . .

Marcel and a Police Superintendent enter

Marcel Come in, Superintendent. (*To Amélie*) I'm sorry chérie, it's the only way.
Policeman (*to others outside*) You two, guard the exits!
Amélie What can I do for you, monsieur?
Policeman A lady! (*To Amélie*) Forgive me, madame. This gentleman here . . . (*To Marcel*) So where is the burglar?
Amélie What burglar?
Policeman I don't know. That's what Monsieur said . . .
Marcel Yes I know I told you that. But if I hadn't then you wouldn't have come. The only thing that's been burgled here is my honour.
Policeman Pardon?
Marcel I would like you to record the presence in this apartment of my wife's lover on the day of our marriage.
Policeman What?
Marcel Go on, record it! Note it down. The unmade bed. Madame's state of undress. (*Taking her wedding dress from the sofa*) Her wedding dress still warm!
Policeman Is this true, madame?
Marcel Do you dare to deny it?
Amélie No I can't. I'd rather a divorce than put up with this mockery of a marriage any longer! Yes monsieur, it's true.
Marcel There!
Policeman And your accomplice?
Amélie He's in the dressing-room! (*Aside*) At least it was with a prince!
Policeman Come out, monsieur! We know you're in there!

The Prince emerges, his hat pulled well down over his face and his cravat up over his chin

Prince I'm coming out!
Marcel Please record the state of Monsieur's dress, or lack of it.

Prince But it was Monsieur here, who threw my clothes out of the window.

Policeman If Monsieur was able to throw them out then you probably weren't wearing them at the time! Your name?

Prince I can't tell you. I'm travelling incognito.

Policeman Pardon?

Marcel He is his Royal Highness the Prince of Palestrie.

Policeman What?

Prince Wretch!

Marcel Note it down, Officer, note it all down!

Policeman Oh no. No, no, no, no!

Marcel What?

Policeman No-no-no-no-no-no-no. A Royal Highness! He's got diplomatic immunity. Tch! Tch! Tch! I don't want to be responsible for creating a diplomatic incident.

Marcel What do you mean?

Policeman Sort yourselves out but don't involve me.

Prince I'm so pleased you understand, Officer.

Marcel But I'm an offended husband.

Policeman How do I know that?

Prince Exactly.

Policeman I know no such thing.

Marcel Of course you do! Look at the state of Madame! The Prince hasn't got any clothes on!

Policeman But you threw them out of the window, monsieur.

Prince Indeed he did!

Marcel That means he wasn't wearing them at the time.

Policeman You call that proof?

Prince Ridiculous!

Marcel And Madame admitted to you herself . . . what else do you need?

Policeman Don't try to teach me my job, monsieur.

Prince Well said!

Policeman Think yourself lucky that I'm not taking your name for making a false accusation to a policeman.

Marcel Me?

Policeman Yes, you! Show me your burglar, monsieur. Go on, show him to me!

Marcel But . . . but . . .

Policeman Yes, well we won't take the matter any further this time.

Prince Bravo!

Marcel I'm a cuckolded criminal!

Policeman Sir! I'm extremely sorry and beg your Highness to accept my humble apologies. It's all this blunderer's fault.

Prince I hereby award you the order of the Commander of Palestrie.

Policeman What me, sir? Oh, sir! What can I say to thank your Highness.

Prince It's nothing. Please leave us.

Policeman Yes sir. (*Bowing*) Sir. Madame. (*To Marcel*) Imbecile!

Marcel What?

Policeman (*off to the others*) Come on you lot. There's no burglar here.

He exits

Amélie Sir, I am so sorry that because of me——!
Prince (*who is extremely rattled*) Never mind! (*To Marcel*) Well, you've certainly made a fine mess of things!
Marcel I suppose you expect me to bow to your might and make my humble apologies!
Prince (*still highly strung*) Tomorrow I shall lodge a complaint at the President's palace!
Marcel Isn't that overdoing it?
Prince I regret that my situation doesn't allow me to mete out your just deserts personally.
Marcel I regret it too, sir.
Prince (*still nervous*) Yes indeed!
Amélie Calm down sir.
Prince (*almost shouting*) I am calm!
Marcel I may as well tell you that I'm very sorry that it happened to be your Highness who got in the way. But I had no choice in the matter.
Prince (*hysterical*) Your conduct is unpermissible!
Amélie It's all Étienne's fault!
Marcel What I wouldn't do to pay him back for this!
Amélie Me too!
Prince Well what are we going to do? I hope you don't expect me to stay here in my smalls? Lend me some of your clothes, so that I can get out of this place.
Marcel But I haven't got any!
Prince Well find some! I don't care what! Give me yours!
Marcel No! Certainly not.

There is a noise outside

Damn!
Prince Who is it?
Étienne (*off*) Are Monsieur and Madame at home?
Marcel It's Étienne!
Amélie He's come to gloat.
Marcel Let him try!

Étienne enters

Étienne Hallo newly-weds!
Amélie You!
Marcel What have you come for?
Étienne Just to see if you were happy together.
Marcel Happy, you wretch! (*He twists Étienne's arm behind his back*)
Étienne Whatever's the matter?
Marcel Have you seen *Have You Anything to Declare* at the Comédie?
Étienne Yes I have. So what?
Marcel We're going to play one of the scenes from it.

Étienne Which one?
Marcel You'll see. Sir? Didn't you say you needed clothes?
Prince On my word I do!
Marcel Good! (*To Étienne*) Your trousers! Give me your trousers!
Étienne What?
Marcel (*pulling a small pistol out of his pocket and aiming it at Étienne*) Your trousers or I'll shoot!
Prince (*finding himself in the line of fire*) Ah!
Étienne You're joking?
Marcel Of course I am. (*He fires in the air*)
Étienne Ah!
Amélie Ah!
Prince Ah!

A piece of ceiling plaster falls to the floor

Amélie My ceiling!
Marcel To hell with your ceiling! (*To Étienne*) Off with your trousers or you'll die like a dog!
Étienne (*begging*) Marcel, please!
Marcel Quickly!
Étienne All right! All right!
Marcel Quicker!
Étienne (*handing his trousers to Marcel*) There they are! There they are!
Marcel (*throwing them to the Prince*) Catch, your Highness!
Prince Thank you! (*Putting them on*) Oh dear! They're going to split!
Marcel Now for your jacket and shirt.
Étienne Come off it, Marcel!
Marcel Are you going to give me your jacket and shirt?
Étienne Here they are! (*Aside*) He's mad, completely mad!
Marcel (*throwing the clothes to the Prince*) Here sir. While you're about it, would you like his underpants?
Prince No thank you! Mine are much nicer.
Étienne Amélie, I beg you!
Amélie It's nothing to do with me.
Marcel And now sir, if you'll forgive me, the scheme I have in mind does not call for the presence of your Highness.
Prince I see! This gentleman is my replacement.
Marcel Got it in one, sir!
Prince I'm more than happy to go. Goodbye and good luck! Goodbye Amélie!
Amélie (*curtsying*) Sir.
Prince (*about to leave he comes back to Étienne*) Cocoi boronzoff Lapetit alagoss!
Étienne What?
Prince Yamolek, Grobouboul!

The Prince exits

Étienne That's too much! He makes off with my clothes and insults me! (*He makes to follow the Prince*) Hey you!

Marcel Don't move! Or I'll fire!

Étienne What do you want of me now?

Marcel What do I want of you? To have you caught *in flagrante delicto* with my wife!

Amélie Precisely!

Marcel You're going to be my wife's lover!

Amélie On the day of her wedding you're going to be discovered with her!

Étienne What?

Marcel Caught with your pants down in the conjugal bedroom!

Amélie Amélie will be discovered in her petticoat!

Étienne (*aside*) They're mad! Mad!

Marcel Now! The Superintendent.

Amélie The Superintendent.

There is a knock at the door

Marcel Who's there?

Policeman (*off*) The Superintendent!

Amélie }
Marcel } (*together*) He's here!

Étienne Ah!

Marcel Come in! Come in, Officer! How timely! We were just talking about you!

The Policeman enters

Policeman About me? Is his Highness still here?

Marcel He's just left.

Policeman I was just bringing him back his clothes which were handed in at the station.

Marcel We'll send them on to him.

Policeman (*seeing Étienne*) Monsieur!

Étienne (*bowing to him*) Monsieur!

Policeman It's the heat, no doubt?

Étienne The heat, yes!

Marcel Why we haven't introduced you! Monsieur Étienne de Milledieu, my best friend: our local policeman! And now, Officer, will you please record that I have just surprised my wife in adulterous *flagrante delicto*.

Policeman What? Again?

Amélie Yes, Officer.

Étienne Marcel please!

Marcel That's enough from you! I was mistaken earlier. My wife's lover wasn't the Prince, it was this gentleman!

Policeman Very handy!

Étienne But it's not true!

Amélie Yes it is, Officer! I recognize him!

Étienne Oh!

Amélie Besides the whole of Paris will tell you it's true.

Étienne Oh!

Policeman Your confession's good enough for me.

Marcel Will you record it please?
Policeman Have you got anything I can write with?
Amélie This way, Officer. (*She goes towards the dressing-room*)
Policeman Coming.
Étienne I protest! This is infamy! I am a citizen of the Republic!
Policeman Oh that doesn't mean a thing, monsieur!

All three exit into the dressing-room

Marcel Revenged at last!

Van Putzeboum enters

Van Putzeboum Goodbye. There you are, little godsonny. I am sorry to interrupt the boom-boom but I have to leave this evening. So I've brought the cheque round.
Marcel The cheque?
Van Putzeboum Your inheritance! You've fulfilled the conditions and here's the money! One million francs of capital plus the compound interest; two hundred and seventy thousand ninety-three francs and five centimes.
Marcel How much?
Van Putzeboum That's the computation.
Marcel Ninety-three francs and five centimes. Perfect!

Amélie comes out of her dressing-room

Amélie The godfather!
Marcel And now, Godfather, I have the honour to announce——
Van Putzeboum Already? I knew it!
Marcel No, no!
Van Putzeboum Oh!
Marcel My forthcoming divorce from Mademoiselle Amélie d'Avranches, Madame Courbois, who I have just caught *in flagrante delicto* with Étienne de Milledieu, my best friend.
Van Putzeboum What?
Marcel (*to Amélie*) Is this true?
Amélie Absolutely.
Van Putzeboum (*trying to take the cheque back*) But then——
Marcel Sorry, Godfather! But haven't the conditions been fulfilled?
Van Putzeboum I think this needs disgusting.
Marcel It certainly is. Your duties as executor are over!

Étienne and the Policeman appear from the dressing-room

Étienne But no, Officer . . .
Policeman I don't care monsieur, I really don't care.
Marcel Time to go, Godfather. Hallo.
Van Putzeboum Goodbye.

Van Putzeboum exits

Étienne (*to Marcel*) This is infamous!
Marcel Goodbye Amélie. (*He kisses her*)

Amélie Goodbye Marcel.
Étienne What about me? What'll become of me?

Marcel takes Amélie and pushes her towards Étienne

Marcel Look mon vieux, keep an eye on Amélie.

   Marcel exits with the Policeman

Étienne What did he say?
Amélie Keep an eye on Amélie.
Étienne Ah!

CURTAIN

FURNITURE AND PROPERTY LIST

ACT I

On stage: Sofa
Side table. *On it:* ashtray, dirty cups
Piano and stool
Table. *On it:* gramophone with record, candles, matches
Card table. *On it:* playing cards
Chairs
Servant's bell
Drinks for **All**

Off stage: Trousers, tunic **(Étienne)**
Coins **(Pochet)**
Large bouquet of flowers **(Florist's Boys)**

Personal: **Bibichon:** lighted cigar, box cigars, matches
Irene: lorgnette
Koshnadieff: coin
Van Putzeboum: cane, ring in pocket

ACT II

On stage: Sofa
Bed with bedding. *Under it:* socks, slippers. *Above it:* night-light
Window curtains with tie-back ropes (closed)
Table. *On it:* dress
Bureau. *On it:* paper, pen, ink, envelopes, candlestick
Bedside table. *On it:* bedside light
Electric bell
Empty champagne bottle, hat, mask, other items of clothing on floor

Off stage: Breakfast tray **(Charlotte)**
Packet of papers and letters, ball of string **(Charlotte)**
2 lighted sparklers, mask **(Amélie)**
Box containing dresses **(Shop Assistant)**
Pair of folded sheets **(Charlotte)**

Personal: **Van Putzeboum:** cane
Prince: letter in pocket
Koshnadieff: coins
Pochet: purse
Étienne: rapier

ACT III

SCENE 1

On stage: Benches
Row of chairs
Podium
Desk
2 tables. *On them:* papers, registers, pens, ink, certificates

Off stage: Cameras **(Photographers)**
Hat **(Pochet)**
Amélie's coat **(Koshnadieff)**

Personal: **Photographers:** cards
Pochet: medal round neck, handkerchief, spectacles in pocket
The Brat: posy of flowers
Marcel: coins in pocket

SCENE 2

On stage: Bed with bedding. *On it:* dressing-gown, **Prince's** clothes
Sofa
Prince's hat, coat, cane, gloves

Off stage: Cheque **(Van Putzeboum)**

Personal: **Marcel:** small pistol in pocket
Van Putzeboum: cane

LIGHTING PLOT

Practical fittings required: night-light above bed, bedside light (Marcel's bedroom)
4 interiors: a salon, 2 bedrooms, a wedding parlour

ACT I Evening
To open: General interior lighting on Amélie's salon
No cues

ACT II Day
To open: Almost total darkness in Marcel's bedroom; night-light on

Cue 1	**Marcel** opens window curtains *Increase lighting*	(Page 27)
Cue 2	**Marcel** turns out night-light *Turn off night-light*	(Page 27)
Cue 3	As **Marcel** closes window curtains *Decrease lighting*	(Page 32)
Cue 4	As **Irene** switches on bedside light *Snap up bedside light*	(Page 33)
Cue 5	As **Irene** lights night-light *Bring up night-light*	(Page 35)
Cue 6	**Irene** switches off bedside light *Snap off bedside light*	(Page 35)
Cue 7	**Amélie** turns out night-light *Turn off night-light*	(Page 37)

ACT III, Scene 1. Day
To open: General interior lighting on wedding parlour
No cues

ACT III, Scene 2. Day
To open: General interior lighting on Amélie's bedroom
No cues

EFFECTS PLOT

ACT I

ACT II

ACT III

Cue 16	**Boas:** "Not long. Good."	(Page 56)
	Music: The Wedding March	
Cue 17	**Mouilletu:** ". . . the ceremony is concluded."	(Page 65)
	Music: The Wedding March	
Cue 18	**Prince:** ". . . so long to get married!"	(Page 69)
	Doorbell rings	
Cue 19	**Amélie:** "I've heard that before!"	(Page 70)
	Doorbell rings	
Cue 20	**Marcel** fires pistol in air	(Page 77)
	Pistol shot, followed by piece of ceiling plaster falling	

Photoset and printed in Great Britain by
The Longdunn Press Ltd., Bristol.